THE OTHER SIDE – A GUIDE TO THE PARANORMAL

The Other Side
A Guide to The Paranormal

Kelly McMullan

JANUS PUBLISHING COMPANY
London, England

First published in Great Britain 2009
by Janus Publishing Company Ltd,
105-107 Gloucester Place,
London W1U 6BY

www.januspublishing.co.uk

British Library Cataloguing-in-Publication Data
A catalogue record for this book is available from the British Library

ISBN 978-1-85756-649-9

Cover Design: Edwin Page

Printed and bound in Great Britain

Contents

Foreword

Paranormal phenomenon is the name given to anything that operates outside and beyond what is considered 'normal' or known.

This description applies to a wide range of phenomena, with hauntings and poltergeist activity making up the majority of reports.

Britain is reputedly the most haunted country in the world, with over 10,000 ghosts, and there are hundreds of documented cases of ghostly sightings, many of which figure in this book.

Throughout my investigation into the paranormal I have been fortunate enough to experience such phenomena as spirit apparitions, orbs and poltergeist activity. The truth is, almost everyone has the ability to experience paranormal phenomena and sometimes it's simply a matter of being in the right place at the right time. However, it is important to keep an open mind, as ghosts generally have to be believed in, in order to be seen and they will rarely appear on command. As well as exploring ghosts, other phenomena are also explained, thereby presenting objective evidence in each category.

It is important to consider all possibilities before deciding whether or not an event is truly paranormal and so with this in mind, each chapter includes the opinions of scientists, psychologists, sceptics and paranormal investigators, thereby weighing up all circumstantial evidence. Most of what you read is the result of extensive research, catalogued reports, eyewitness accounts and personal experience. I hope you enjoy reading this book as much as I have enjoyed writing it and that you will feel inspired to have a go at investigating some spooky locations for yourself!

1

Ghosts and Hauntings

For anybody who has ever thought about life after death, one thing nearly always comes to mind: ghosts. There has always been a fascination with the possibility that we are not alone and that we all have a soul, which survives the death of the external body.

Many ancient civilisations believed in life after death or in reincarnation and some, such as the ancient Egyptians, worshipped many different gods. Modern-day religions also teach that after death, the soul is judged and if the individual was good when they were alive, then they shall reap the benefits in a paradise or heaven in the afterlife.

Ghosts can be defined as souls that are earthbound, mostly appearing in the dwelling in which they lived when they were alive. There are several theories to explain the appearance of ghosts. Sometimes, it is the case that they simply do not want to leave, while others cannot. If they were murdered, committed suicide or died in an accident, when the soul leaves the body they often do not realise that they are, in fact, dead, thereby preventing the soul from moving on. Some may be unhappy, seeking in death to put right the wrongs they did in life, whilst others may be afraid of judgement and therefore remain grounded.

There is often some confusion about the differences between spirits and ghosts. Spirits are often thought of as being the same as ghosts; however, this is not the case. Spirits more often than not pass over and embrace the light. A distinguishing feature is that spirits appear to hover and float about 3 feet above the ground, whereas earthbound ghosts appear at ground level.

Spirits are able to visit the places they frequented in life and see their loved ones, whilst at the same time being able to return to the spirit world, as they are not bound to one particular place.

There are numerous ghosts among us here on Earth, because unlike spirits, they refuse to move on for various reasons. It is often the case that they can't understand what mortals are doing in their 'space' and some may even become malevolent.

It is a popular myth that ghosts are simply transparent entities that float in mid-air and although this is a feature for a certain number of sightings, the majority of apparitions appear solid and three-dimensional. Ghosts can also take on other forms, which will be explored in the next chapter.

2

Types of Ghost

Presences:

Most people report seeing a presence, rather than an 'apparition'. It may be that in a particular room, they feel that they are being watched by an unseen entity, or they may experience a distinct smell, such as flowers, which appears to follow them from room to room. There is a close link between presences and poltergeists.

Anniversary Ghosts:

These ghosts are reputed to appear at a specific time, date or anniversary of a particular incident. For example, a person who was murdered often returns to the location of their death on the anniversary of that day. Soldiers who died in battle can also be seen at certain times, in locations such as castles, re-enacting battles. More commonly, anniversary ghosts generally appear about the same time of year as opposed to on the actual date, owing to atmospheric conditions.

Poltergeists:

Where ghosts are understood as being apparitions haunting particular places, poltergeists are thought to haunt people.

Commonly, poltergeists are drawn to a particular individual and while ghosts stay in one locality, poltergeists can move about and have even been known to follow people.

Manifestations such as moving furniture, objects flying through the air, loud noises and even anomalous voices can occur.

Activity can persist in a finite time span of perhaps weeks, months or even a year.

Interactive Ghosts:

A different entity to 'conventional' ghosts and not showing the violence of poltergeists, interactive ghosts form the principal evidence that there is survival of the soul after death.

Interactive ghosts are aware of your presence and may communicate with you, follow you and even identify themselves.

These ghosts seem to only appear randomly.

Time Slips:

What may seem to be an 'interactive ghost' may in fact be what is described as a time slip. Here, there are situations where a 'window' of opportunity opens up between two time periods, thus allowing people on either side to see each other.

Sometimes, there is a shift in their surroundings, thus enabling people to 'see' them as they once were in the past.

Ghosts of the living (doubles, doppelgängers, vardogers and bi-locations):

In this instance, a perception of a ghost is actually a person, who is still very much alive. Doubles occur when a person is seen in two places at the same time by different people.

Doppelgängers appear nearby the real person and are often found to be carrying out the same acts. Vardogers are forerunners in time. In other words, a person may visit a location for the first time, only to find that they are recognised by other people, even though they do not recognise them in return (unlike déjà vu, where the person senses that they have been to that particular place, or carried out a certain act, before).

Bi-locations occur when a person appears to divide themselves between two locations.

Ghosts of the dying (crisis apparitions):

Crisis apparitions bridge the gap between the survival of the spirit and out-of-body experiences. Some crisis apparitions have been said to have alerted people to dangerous situations.

There is also evidence to suggest that on the brink of death, people have appeared to their friends or relatives to alert them.

It may, however, also be that some form of telepathy is taking place – a subject explored by the Swiss psychologist Carl Jung.

Haunted Objects:

These are not much different to haunted places, except for the fact that they are movable. There have been many reports of haunted cars, mirrors, furniture and even, in one case, a haunted biscuit container. Such objects will tend to be passed on to different owners over a period of time; therefore, subsequent owners will report the same phenomena as the previous owners.

Phantom Hitch-Hikers:

Ghosts such as phantom hitch-hikers display the same characteristics as interactive ghosts. Reports often describe picking up a person on a lonely stretch of road, only to find the person 'vanish' from their car shortly afterwards.

3

Haunted North-West England

Living in the north-west of England, I have researched and compiled a list of haunted 'hot spots' in this particular region.

They range from halls and country houses, to nightclubs and pubs, and all have a plethora of ghosts.

Chingle Hall – Goosnargh, near Longridge, Lancashire:

Chingle Hall has become famously notorious for its paranormal activity over the decades. It is situated on a former Viking settlement and the original manor house was built by Adam de Singleton in 1260 and many of its original features still remain.

Legend has it that any person who had committed a crime could flee to Chingle Hall for protection, providing that they wore white clothing and used the 'sanctuary knocker' three times. The priest would then come to the door to listen to their confession, where they were then given nine days' respite in which time they could escape.

The hall is associated with four martyred Catholic saints and these days it is popular with paranormal investigators, psychics and mediums. Over twenty ghosts have been identified in and around Chingle Hall, including ghostly monks, a nun, Victorian children, a grey lady, a cavalier, a Roman centurion, a knight, a colonel, a phantom cat and many more. Incidents include 'white mist' appearing in visitors' photographs, as well as figures of monks having been captured on camera.

Overpowering aromas of incense and lavender have been experienced in the chapel and visitors describe being pushed, pinched or having their hair pulled. Heavy footsteps have been heard all around the building and the sound of children crying, as well as the sound of ringing bells, and sudden drops in temperature have also been noted.

In November 1995, members of the Alphelion Ghost Research Society carried out an investigation at Chingle Hall. They recorded 'a sudden onset of oppressive headaches', scratching noises, a reported sighting of the figure of a monk and sudden drops in temperature.

Robert Appleton (ghost hunter) believes that much of the paranormal activity occurs as a result of the fact that the hall is built on crossed ley lines – paths of magnetic earth energy that attracts spiritual activity. He has a collection of photographs taken in and around Chingle displaying manifestations such as vortices, grotesque faces and what appears to be a cloven hoof.

Bramall Hall – Bramhall, Stockport, Cheshire:

The Manor of Bramale as it was once called is recorded in the Domesday Book. In 1935, the house was sold to the local council and was opened to the public the following year. It is full of hidden passageways, paintings and filled-in doorways. In the 1630s, on New Year's Eve, the legendary 'Red Rider of Bramall Hall' stayed for a night. However, the following morning, the owner of the house, William Davenport, was found dead and the mysterious traveller had vanished. Hundreds of years later, locals have reported seeing a figure with a 'billowing red cape' riding through the courtyard on each anniversary of Mr Davenport's murder on New Year's Eve.

This is not the only ghost said to haunt Bramall Hall: a 'lady in white', whose lover was murdered by robbers, is said to appear in certain rooms within the building. She is understood to have committed suicide and her apparition has been seen to be seemingly 'walking through a wall'. When the wall was taken down, a doorway was found that had been previously sealed up.

Heathercliffe Country House – Frodsham, Warrington, Cheshire:

Heathercliffe was built in the 1860s and the surrounding grounds were used in 1991 to film part of the set for Robin Hood. It was only in the 1970s that Heathercliffe House showed any signs of being haunted. Before the house was turned into a hotel, a group of students stayed there as guests in the residence and one evening, they started playing on an ouija board. Later that same night, they saw something 'terrifying' and fled from the building.

Still today, staff and guests note a presence, objects move around and disappear and guests often complain of a feeling that they are being watched.

Lyme Park – Disley, Cheshire:

Lyme Park is the largest house in Cheshire. The interior includes ceiling paintings by Leoni, intricate tapestries, woodcarvings and stunning sculptures. It is set within beautiful grounds extending to 1,400 acres and it was the family home of the Leighs for 600 years, until taken over in 1946 by the National Trust; it is now part-financed by Stockport Borough Council. Occasionally, a phantom funeral procession is seen proceeding up a small hill, known as Knight's Low, Buxton Road, and behind it walks the 'woman in white'. This is a phantom re-enactment of the funeral cortège of Sir Piers Leigh, who died in Paris on 16 June 1422 of wounds sustained in the Battle of Meux. His body was brought back to Cheshire for burial and is said to have rested for a short while at Knight's Low.

The lady in white is not his widow, but his mistress Blanche, who is said to have died from grief after hearing the tragic news of his death. The spirit of the 'woman in white' has been seen at the site where Sir Piers Leigh was buried and also in the sixteenth-century manor house. The affected area is known as the 'ghost room' and members of staff have seen the figure of the tall woman in a white gown beneath one of the huge trees in front of the building.

Later on, during an excavation, a skeleton was found inside the Hall under the floorboards of a secret room – it is believed that these are the remains of a priest. The ghostly apparition of this priest has been seen walking along a corridor outside the room and the sound of ringing bells has also been heard on occasion. The secret room was later discovered to be the one that Mary Queen of Scots slept in whilst imprisoned at Lyme Hall.

Manchester Cathedral – Central Manchester:

A headless dog is said to have haunted the streets of Central Manchester in the early part of the nineteenth century. It was seen many times in the vicinity of the old church, which is now Manchester Cathedral. These days, there have been a few sightings of a 'black shadow' disappearing behind the cathedral.

Warrington – Cheshire:

On 22 July 1998, some noisy ghosts making life a misery for a family in Orford, Warrington, were exorcised from the house by the psychic Kevin McGrath, who says he had found 'the spirit of a man, who had committed suicide in the house fifteen years before, a little fair-haired girl aged around 9 years old and an elderly grandfather', who he believes was the owner's own grandfather.

On 14 March 1997, the Warrington psychic Kevin McGrath removed the ghost of a pinstripe-suited man from a town centre house after the spirit was seen following the owner around the building.

Helen Syers of Beatty Avenue, Orford, Warrington was driving along Long lane, when she saw a round, disc-like object floating above the trading estate. 'It was moving in an erratic zigzag movement', she said, 'and it was marked with red lights and one white light'. Could this have been a possible UFO sighting?

The Kings Head Public House – Bolton, Lancashire:

Recently, there has been a lot of paranormal activity associated with this pub. Doors are often said to have slammed shut by themselves and the landlord was once awoken by an oppressive atmosphere that suddenly flooded through his bedroom. The pub is said to be built on top of a graveyard and the haunting is thought to be caused by phantom Cavaliers.

The Coach & Horses Public House – Chester, Cheshire:

This Tudor building, formerly a coaching house, is situated on Northgate Street and is said to be home to a rather mischievous poltergeist. The majority of incidents have taken place recently, with regular drinkers at the pub reporting to have seen ashtrays move across tabletops by themselves. Other witnesses have claimed to have seen strange blue lights flashing from within the walls.

There was also an incident in 1988, when an elderly gent came into the pub late one summer's evening. He told the barmaid that his wife had passed away suddenly and being perturbed by all the memories within his home, he asked if he could have a room for the night. The gentleman said that he would be taking a brisk walk around the town before returning later on. When midnight came and went, the management became concerned as to his whereabouts. At two o'clock in the morning they contacted the police, giving them the gentleman's name and address. The police then went round to his house to see if he had returned there in a confused state, but upon speaking to the neighbours, they were astonished to discover that shortly after the man's wife had died, he, too, had passed away, seemingly of a broken heart.

What the bar staff had seen that night was, in fact, his spirit returning to the pub he once frequented when he was alive.

Shakespeare Hotel – Manchester City Centre, Lancashire:

Much mystery surrounds this pub situated on Fountain Street in the centre of Manchester. Originally named The Shambles, this Tudor pub was actually built in Chester in 1656. It was later moved to Manchester in the 1920s and its resident ghost appeared to move with it. She is said to have been a kitchen maid, who died in the nineteenth century after being raped by the chef. He later committed suicide and the marks on the beam from which he hanged himself can still be seen.

Interestingly, the site upon which the pub was relocated is where a young maid died from spontaneous human combustion, a strange phenomenon in itself.

The hotel is now home to the ghostly girl, who has been seen on several occasions, with most sightings being reported in the 1970s. She has been spotted standing at the top of a flight of stairs, once appearing to be on fire. Other witnesses more recently have reported suddenly feeling 'hot' for no apparent reason, when standing in certain parts of the building, and upon entering the kitchen area, some have been said to have been overcome by feelings of sadness.

The Blue Bell Inn – Northgate Street, Chester, Cheshire:

The Blue Bell is the oldest domestic building in the City of Chester and in 1494, the pub was known as The Bell. The Blue Bell's ghost is known by staff and locals as 'Henrietta', believed to have once been the sweetheart of a Royalist soldier during the Civil War. On the eve of the battle of Rowton Moor in 1645, Henrietta waved goodbye to her soldier. However, sadly, he did not return from battle and by nightfall, Henrietta had tragically taken her own life in the cellar.

Staff have reported seeing her ghost climb the cellar steps and walk through walls and visitors have sometimes felt something invisible 'brush past' them. She has also been seen at the upstairs window, where she is said to have watched and waited for her lover to return.

The Bulls Head – Swinton, Manchester, Lancashire:

This building dates back to the sixteenth century, but was rebuilt in 1826. It is situated opposite St Peters church and graveyard and many accounts of paranormal activity are reported to have taken place here. Strange noises, objects being moved, cold spots and apparitions appearing in the cellar have all been witnessed.

In one terrifying instance whilst in the cellar, the manager's stepfather was attacked, resulting in a nasty gash over his right eye that required eight stitches. He claims that as he was about to leave the cellar, a hand had gripped his left shoulder and a voice had whispered his name harshly in his ear. Shortly after this he was found by his family lying on the floor bleeding.

Prior to this incident, both he and his friend had witnessed several orange and red lights appearing and shortly afterwards, some barrels in the adjacent room had reportedly begun to move.

Ye Olde Man & Scythe – Bolton, Lancashire:

A number of paranormal events have been witnessed here. In the late twentieth century, a woman drinking in this public house found her hands suddenly covered in blood as she was about to leave, although there were no apparent wounds of her own and no other source for the liquid could be found. More recently, activity such as people being pinched, women's skirts being tugged at and objects being moved have also been reported. This is said to be caused by an 8-year-old spirit girl called Geny. A phantom dog has also been spotted running around in the museum room.

Brannigans – Deansgate, Manchester, Lancashire:

There have been several cases of supernatural activity reported to have taken place in this nightclub. Bar staff have experienced phenomena such as cold spots, bottles and glasses being hurled around the upstairs bar and, on occasion, the spooky sound of chanting has also been heard. It is believed that there was once a monastery on this site and the monks who once inhabited the monastery are believed to have been unhappy, because of the fact that their monastery is now a noisy nightclub. It is also believed that there are remains buried beneath the building.

Butterflies Nightclub – Oldham, Lancashire:

This case was investigated by paranormal researcher Peter Hough. He states that one night, 'The alarms had gone off and the police contacted the manager'. The police accompanied him inside and there appeared to be no sign of forced entry.

The men later checked the security camera and saw a figure walking down the corridor and through a locked door. The building is Victorian and a man was believed to have died there whilst carrying out renovation work.

The Big Bar – Warrington, Cheshire:

It has been noted that in this nightclub, and also in the restaurant next door to it, there have been bouts of poltergeist activity.

Chairs have been seen balancing on top of one another, objects have been hurled around the rooms, the sounds of heavy footsteps have been heard and objects such as keys going missing and reappearing elsewhere have been noted. It seems the attacks proved too much for the manager, who left sometime shortly after the activity began.

WA1 Nightclub – Warrington, Cheshire:

Both myself and employees of WA1 have experienced paranormal activity within this building. Glasses have been seen balancing on the bar, bottle tops have been seen popping off by themselves and objects have been known to move, later turning up elsewhere. Managers have felt their clothing being tugged at and the appearance of a female apparition dressed in Victorian clothing has also been sighted. The building is believed to have once been a factory, so it could be a possibility that somebody died there many years ago.

4

Haunted Houses

Haunted houses have been the centre of interest for paranormal researchers for many years. When a building earns itself the reputation for being haunted, manifestations do not necessarily occur all the time. Some ghosts only appear at around the time of their death, such as anniversary ghosts, and some people appear to 'trigger off' ghostly phenomena more than others.

There are two main 'types' of haunted house: those in which the occupiers describe feeling or seeing a presence, or perhaps even experiencing poltergeist activity, and those that have ley lines running through the building, thus allowing access for spirits, or even triggering supernatural activity. People who are gifted with psychic abilities appear to be able to open this 'gateway' and let spirits enter the home subconsciously.

There have been several, if not hundreds, of accounts of haunted houses all over the world. Examples of manifestations include apparitions, items being moved, interference with electrical/electronic equipment, disembodied voices, significant changes in temperature, strange or unusual odours and the sound of footsteps. There are many infamous haunted houses, one of which is Borley Rectory – the most haunted house in England.

The haunting of Borley Rectory on the Essex/Suffolk border during the 1920s and 1930s is undoubtedly one of the most famous in Britain. The rectory was built in 1863 on the site of an old Benedictine monastery for the Reverend HDE Bull and his family. From around 1885, there were sightings of a ghostly nun in the grounds of the rectory and poltergeist activity was experienced not only by the Bull family, but by all the previous occupiers who had lived there. A later investigation uncovered buried bones, believed to be that of a nun, and a seance revealed that she had been strangled on the site 300 years earlier.

Phantom footsteps were often heard and even a phantom coach and horses was seen by Mr and Mrs Edward Cooper, who once lived in the cottage near to the rectory.

In 1927, Reverend Bull passed away in the 'blue room'. This was later to become noted as the most haunted room in the rectory. In 1928, Reverend Eric Smith and his wife moved in and they complained of hearing ghostly voices, and objects were noted as disappearing. Many other residents of the rectory, such as Marianne Foyster, described glasses being smashed, stone throwing, mysterious writing appearing on walls and, in one terrifying instance, being thrown from her bed by some strange force or other. In the 1930s, the building was investigated by Harry Price, who was accused of exaggerating; however, it is unfair to say that he invented the phenomena, as the occurrences were happening long before he came on the scene. The rectory was gutted by a fire in 1939 and was eventually demolished in 1944; however, the paranormal activity did not cease and to this day, people have described seeing apparitions on the grounds where the rectory once stood.

Another infamous haunted house that almost everybody is familiar with is Amityville, on Ocean Avenue in Amityville, New York, and has never been short of media attention. In the late 1970s, the publication of *The Amityville Horror* by Jay Anson became a best-seller and was later turned into a blockbuster film with several sequels.

Amityville told the story of the Lutz family and their experience after moving into the house in December 1975.

They claimed to have experienced temperature drops, swarms of flies in the sewing room, foul stenches, green slime exuding from the walls and levitation and apparitions of demonic entities, amongst other things. They even claimed that their personalities had changed whilst living in the house.

These strange phenomena were allegedly connected to the previous occupier Ronald DeFeo, who slaughtered his family while they slept in the house on 14 November 1974.

Family friend and priest Father Ray is said to have blessed the house before the Lutz family moved in. He was heard to have turned to Mr George Lutz and said, 'You know, I felt something really strange in that one upstairs bedroom.' The bedroom in question was the one that had once belonged to Robert DeFeo and was later to become the Lutz's sewing room – the most haunted room in the house.

The haunting, although just 'cold spots' and creaking noises to begin with, soon began to escalate. Doors started to slam shut on their own and there was the strange sound of a marching band in the middle of the night, although no television or radio was switched on at the time. It wasn't long before the Lutz family began to hear more footsteps throughout the house and after they discovered a small hidden room in the basement, which was painted red, the paranormal activity really began to intensify.

The family's dog Harry, upon nearing the room, backed away and began to cower. This was the first time, according to the family, that their dog had ever behaved in such a manner.

It wasn't long before the Lutzes' 4-year-old daughter Missy also became affected. She became withdrawn and talked about her 'imaginary friend' called Jodie. This was to be the entity that the Lutz's later saw in the form of a demonic-looking pig hovering outside the windows at night. It was also the name of one of the DeFeo children, who had been murdered.

Eventually, the haunting became so bad that the Lutz family decided to try to bless the house once again, this time by doing it themselves. The first time they attempted to do this, their eldest son Danny's hands became 'trapped' in the window, which could not be explained, as the window was not one that could easily slam down, and especially not by itself. His hands were badly swollen and yet when his parents were about to leave the house to take him to hospital, the boy's hands miraculously returned to normal. Upon the second attempt to bless the house, they heard voices telling them to stop. It was after this that things really began to get unbearable for the family. In one frightening instance, Mr Lutz described how his wife had begun to levitate off the bed and at the same time, he had felt something 'get into bed' with him. The children's beds in the next room could be heard slamming and sliding up and down across the floor, the lights in their room began to flicker on and off and their dog started to vomit profusely.

The next morning, the Lutz family went to stay at Mrs Kathy Lutz's mother's house. The entities, however, appeared to have followed them and they experienced levitations, apparitions and nightmares during that night. In March 1976, paranormal investigators, a photographer, a news crew and researchers from Duke University came to investigate the house. They each came at different times throughout the day and night and some even stayed overnight. They conducted a seance and concluded that whatever was responsible for the haunting had never been human – the entities were of a 'demonic' nature and an Anglican or Roman Catholic priest was needed in order to cleanse the property, but when a Catholic priest came to exorcise the house, he was told to 'get out' by a gruff, disembodied voice. It wasn't long after this incident that the Lutz family packed their bags and left for San Diego to start a new life.

The occurrences were said to be very much hyped and almost certainly exaggerated. This is not to say, however, that paranormal activity did not occur. There were several witnesses to the events, such as those encountered by both of the priests who visited the house, and those experienced by friends of the family, who heard footsteps upstairs on several occasions, even though all of the adults were downstairs at the time and the children were asleep in bed. To this day, there is much speculation as to what caused the paranormal activity in 112 Ocean Avenue.

Some say the spirits were those of the family that DeFeo had murdered, whilst others believe the entities were of a demonic nature and could well have been responsible for 'possessing' DeFeo and ordering him to murder his family. Indeed, this was declared by DeFeo himself, who claimed that the 'evil creature' had controlled him. Could it have been that his family members were put into some kind of 'trance'? Though none of the other family members were woken by the previous gunshots and he had not used a silencer. Some sceptics still claim that the whole story was a hoax; however, this does not explain why several people, including two priests, would feel the need to lie about something like this. The mystery surrounding the 'red' room has yet to be solved.

It is regarded that one of the most notorious haunted houses in Britain is, in fact, a public house – The Ancient Ram Inn in the Cotswolds. This eerie inn lies in the country town of Wotton-under-Edge, Gloucestershire, and has been subject to a number of paranormal experiences. The Ram Inn was built in 1189 and has a very interesting history. It is believed to have witnessed black magic rituals, child sacrifice and suicide and it has even been the hideout of highwaymen in years gone by.

During excavation work, many secrets of the past were uncovered. Among the findings were a bricked-up tunnel that led to the church opposite, a priest hole, a hidden grave and the most macabre of all, the discovery of a mass burial ground beneath the floor of one of the rooms. This latter discovery was unearthed by a local dowser, who sensed the presence of bodies beneath the foundations. Following this, an archaeologist dug up the floor and discovered the bones of several children, along with two broken ceremonial daggers. It was later uncovered that the site was once a pagan burial ground, where many children were sacrificed during pagan rituals.

There have been numerous accounts by witnesses who claim to have experienced paranormal activity within The Ram Inn.

Indeed, the owner himself claims that he has seen dark shadows and apparitions in the so called 'Bishop's room', which is considered to be one of the most spiritually active rooms in the UK, with stories of orbs, apparitions, noises, a ghostly cat and possession being just some. He has also reported being dragged out of bed by an unseen force that he believes to be an incubus.

Many visitors who have stayed overnight have reportedly fled in terror after feeling a sensation of 'something creeping into bed with them' and eight people who have slept in this room have had to be exorcised.

Other phenomena within the building include items being moved, objects 'floating' around rooms, electrical equipment being operated by themselves, disembodied voices, the appearance of a strange mist, apparitions and orbs (most frequently spotted in the barn), as well as people being touched and even physically attacked. The building is also situated on ley lines, which are said to attract negative energies.

The Ram Inn attracts many investigators and paranormal researchers and it was during one such investigation by Living TV's Most Haunted team that many things were discovered about the inn's past. Spiritualist medium Derek Acorah immediately picked up on evil spirits upon entering the building. The presence of a witch was detected, whose accomplice is a large black cat said to be the witch's 'familiar'.

During the investigation, the sound of a cat was heard on an MP3 recording, even though there were no physical cats actually present in the building. On several occasions, guests have reported hearing the sound of a cat's miaow and some have even seen the black cat prowling around the building.

Also detected were the ghosts of a malevolent monk and priest, said to have been responsible for the sacrifice of many people, mostly children, during pagan rituals. During the team's night vigils, Stuart Torevell, who is responsible for camera rigs on set, was violently attacked by an angry spirit. He was physically pushed to the ground and punched repeatedly in the stomach, which left him and the other team members extremely traumatised. Stuart claims it was this incident that caused the onset of alopecia. Some years ago, an attempt by a local priest to exorcise these evil spirits failed when he was forced to his knees by one of the spirits and he eventually fled from the building in terror, unable to finish the exorcism.

There have been several other investigations and vigils held by paranormal and psychic investigators in this property, in which photographs were taken on several occasions, depicting strange light anomalies, such as orbs and floating red lights (said to signify an evil presence); sudden temperature drops were also detected and rapping sounds were captured on recording equipment. Overall, there is vast evidence to suggest that the Ancient Ram Inn is home to many different spirits, most of which appear to be malevolent, and it was once the scene of notably some of the most horrific events to have taken place in the country.

List of paranormal activity associated with a haunted house:

- Items being moved from one place to another.
- The disappearance of objects that usually turn up in a different place.
- Objects levitating in mid-air.
- Cold spots and temperature drops.
- Interference of electrical equipment, such as lights, television, stereo, etc.
- The feeling that you are being watched.
- Doors opening and closing by themselves.
- Noises, such as banging, rapping and scratching.
- The sound of footsteps.
- Whispering, gruff, disembodied voices.
- Smells, ranging from strong perfume to foul odours.

- The appearance of orbs.
- The appearance of mist/ectoplasm.
- Apparitions.

Ghostly Animals

If human spirits survive death, then surely animals would also.

However, although there have been reported sightings of domestic pets, such as cats and dogs, returning to their owners after their death, there have been no known reports of intellectual creatures, such as dolphins and whales, doing so.

The concept of 'animal heaven' or the existence of animal spirits is a difficult one. What about insects, for example? They are living creatures: would they not survive after death? Some explanations offered by investigators of the paranormal are that 'lesser' creatures have a group soul, whilst more humanised animals have a soul like ours. It seems that cats and dogs are more likely to appear, because they are close companions to humans, although there have been a few sightings of phantom horses and birds.

Most common of all are sightings of the 'black dogs', which form the most frequently reported 'ghost animals' across the UK.

Many believe that these dogs are the devil, whilst others claim that they are witches' familiars – an animal that is said to carry out instructions given by a witch. Black dogs have long been associated with death. In ancient Egypt, the god Anubis, who guided the dead to the underworld, was depicted with a black jackal's head. Similar to this was the three-headed dog Cerberus, who featured in Greek mythology as guarding the Greek realm of the dead. Numerous accounts of black dog sightings involve witnesses claiming that the dogs appear to have glowing red eyes.

They are also said to disappear suddenly and to have the ability to change in size and appearance.

Derbyshire is renowned for its ghostly black dog sightings.

Barghasts, as they are known, are black dogs said to be about half the size of a calf, with a shaggy black coat. Their name literally means 'the spirit of the funeral' and they are said to forewarn of impending death and disaster. They are believed to live all over the Peak District and in the past, lead miners connected certain accidents with sightings of one of these black dogs.

There have been many sightings of a phantom, large dog in the grounds of Hermitage farmhouse, a 300-year-old building situated in Ipstones, Derby. The dog is said to have been seen at the end of the lane leading to the farm and a man is alleged to have kicked at the beast, only for his boot to touch nothing as the dog vanished into thin air.

During the Jacobite Rebellion of 1745, Bonnie Prince Charles' Scottish soldiers were led south, eventually turning back at Derby after a massacre claimed the lives of almost every soldier. The ghosts of black dogs have been sighted along the route, allegedly guarding the soldiers' graves.

There have been frequent reports of a black phantom dog appearing in Peel Castle on the Isle of Man and many frightened witnesses have reported hearing doglike howls emanating from the guardrooms. It is believed that the dog dates back from early pagan rituals. Another dog that is frequently spotted is Black Shuck, a Norfolk black dog with one eye, that witnesses say glows red and 'burns like a lantern'.

When he appears, he is often surrounded by burning flames and a smell of brimstone.

Possibly the most horrific black dog encounter ever recorded took place in Bungay, Suffolk, on the morning of Sunday 4 August 1577. During a violent thunderstorm, while many of the townsfolk were in church, a black dog suddenly appeared. The dog, illuminated by the lightning flashes, was witnessed by everyone inside the church. It is said to have run down the central aisle, striking dead two people who had been praying, breaking the church clock and scratching the stone and metal work on the door in the process. This event is recorded on the market weathervane, which depicts a grotesque, demonic black dog.

A similar black dog is also said to have appeared only 7 miles away in a church in Blythburgh, in which three people were killed and several others were left injured and disturbed by the incident. Marks on the church door were also clearly visible and many believe that both incidents are linked. Although the majority of black dog incidents occur in the UK, there are also some reported sightings in other parts of the world that appear to strike an uncanny resemblance. During the Middle Ages on the Island of Sicily, people believed that the 'plague death' appeared as the image of a large black dog. It was said to enter their churches and once inside, it allegedly smashed ornaments and desecrated altars. Many claimed to have seen it and furthermore, they believed that when it appeared, somebody was sure to die a sudden death.

It could be argued that reports such as this are not necessarily paranormal, for there was a strong belief in superstition during the periods in which these events were recorded. Diseases such as the plague were rife at the time and as nobody really understood where they came from, it was easier to put the blame onto something, possibly a rabid dog that happened to find its way into the church at that particular time. However, it is important to note that there are some recent reports of black dog sightings that seem to display all the evidence to suggest they are genuine animal spirits, such as the phantom hound that haunts Peel Castle.

Indeed, one reason put forward explaining why the majority of 'animal ghost' cases involve domestic pets is that the great love of an animal, or the constant grieving of the loss of a pet, will often have an effect on the animal similar to that of a human spirit, who may have experienced a sudden, violent or tragic death. This often tends to be one of the reasons as to why many human spirits return and such emotions could feasibly also make the animals return to their owners for a short period of time.

Another contributing factor could be the close bond between owner and pet; however, unlike human spirits, ghostly animals rarely interact with humans.

Ghosts on computer and TV screens

As modern technology is becoming more advanced these days, it's hardly surprising that there are more cases of supernatural activity involving electronic equipment than ever before. The most popular electronic devices affected by such phenomena appear to be televisions and computers. There are a number of reports by people claiming to have witnessed such things as the television changing channels seemingly by itself or being switched off altogether and in some cases, even the frightening appearance of demonic faces on the screen after it has been switched off have been known to occur.

An example of such a case took place in Farmington, Maine, USA, where the residents Bernie and Sylvia Howard experienced many kinds of paranormal phenomena, such as the disappearance of objects and noises such as footsteps and bangs, but perhaps one of the most macabre incidents involved the couple's television. In the year of 1984, the couple and two of their friends were watching television in the living room, when suddenly the picture changed. The film they had been watching had vanished and instead of the normal screen, there was now a blank screen depicting a blue colour in its place.

A few seconds later, an elderly woman's face appeared on the screen, remaining there for around thirty seconds, after which it disappeared and the movie came back on. The viewers of this strange event thought nothing of it, putting it down to signal interference; however, twenty minutes later, it happened again.

This time, Mr Howard switched over to another channel and yet the face remained on the screen for around thirty seconds, before disappearing again.

A couple of weeks passed and the face continued to appear, but this time on another television set in another room, which had also started to switch itself on and off. Eventually, the Howard's contacted the television repairman, who reported no fault in the set whatsoever. That same night, the experience became even more eerie, when the face appeared again. In this instance, the woman's lips began to move and an electronically disembodied voice was emitted from the television, although it was so distorted and static that the residents could not make out the words. Stranger still, after this event, the haunting stopped and to this day, nobody can offer a suitable explanation as to the cause of this strange occurrence.

This case, as eerie as it may seem, is not unfamiliar. There have been numerous reports of such events taking place and even a few photographs depicting faces on a television screen have been taken, although whether or not these are all genuine is another matter. A particularly extraordinary story took place in Swansea, south Wales. The man who lived here reported that whilst watching television late one night and after the station he had been watching went off air, his television set had tuned in to an unknown station. As this occurred, he heard hissing noises and static, which was not unusual in itself; however, just as he was about to turn the television off, he caught sight of his recently deceased dog on the screen. He was unable to come to a satisfactory conclusion as to what the cause was, although some sceptics claim that he may have been tired and whilst on the brink of sleep, his brain had produced the hallucination. The man, however, remains adamant that what he saw was, indeed, a vision of his deceased dog.

Computers are now very much a part of everyday life and most homes nowadays have one. There have been many strange accounts involving paranormal activity and the computer – as in one particular case, where the home of a man became invaded by a poltergeist. The usual things occurred, such as objects being moved, and in one instance, the man returned home from work to find that all of his coat hangers had been taken out of his wardrobe and had been neatly lined up on his bed. However, it wasn't long before the poltergeist found a new way of playing tricks. The man enjoyed playing a game of scrabble on his computer, which involved making words from the letters that were dealt. As the man did not have a 'partner' to play with, the computer became his opponent.

Things began to get disturbing though, when words started to appear that directly related to his life. Some might say that this could have been entirely coincidental; however, another report similar to this one occurred in the home of Mr Ken Webster that seemed to defy explanation.

Mr Webster wrote about his experiences in his book *The Vertical Plane*, having moved into a new cottage on the Cheshire/north Wales border, at which point he first began to experience poltergeist activity. Events ranged from furniture being piled on top of one another to messages being scrawled onto walls and floors. Stranger still were the messages that started to appear on the family's Acorn computer. In the course of two years, over 300 messages appeared, witnessed by many different people, such as relatives, friends and even visitors. The messages seemed to be from previous occupiers of the cottage and in one strange instance, a message appeared bearing the inscription 2109, which some researchers state could be evidence of a spirit travelling forwards in time.

Many researchers investigated the phenomenon and seemed to be impressed with what they saw, deeming it to be a genuine paranormal case. In other instances while the researchers were present, visionary phenomena manifested on the computer screen, such as a picture showing the plan of the cottage from the sixteenth century, coupled with strange messages similar to those that appeared on the walls and floors of the cottage. Confirmation as to the accuracy of the messages has since emerged; however, the case remains inconclusive. Some sceptics have argued that this could simply be the work of computer hackers, although this does not explain how they could have known the detailed descriptions of the cottage, not to mention being able to draw maps, and it also does not account for the weird writing appearing on the walls.

Some scientists offer an interesting theory on the matter, claiming that as with poltergeist sightings, they are often triggered by an individual's high levels of electromagnetic energy.

Electronic equipment is easily scrambled by electrical fields; therefore people who possess high amounts of electricity in their bodies may cause interference akin to the spontaneous psychokinesis (PK) that is found to be present in poltergeist cases. Paranormal investigators, however, add that such reports are increasing as technology grows ever more sophisticated and because spirits seem to be attracted to electrical sources, they may find this to be an alternative way in which to communicate with the living.

Poltergeists:

> 'On 12 March 1985, the occupants of a house in Aboro, a district in the City of Abidjan (which was once capital of the Ivory Coast in West Africa) had the terrifying experience of seeing blood spurt from their walls. It drenched clothes, pots and pans in the kitchen, the shower and some of the doors.
>
> Even more grotesque was the occurrence of bloody footprints when the occupants moved around the house. Not a single person was wounded or injured in any way'. (Source of quote – Stone. R. *Poltergeists and the Paranormal*, Blitz Editions, 1993).

This may sound like something out of a horror movie, but it is, in fact, a noted case of poltergeist activity. There have been many other similar cases to this strange and horrific occurrence, such as that reported by a couple in Atlanta, Georgia. In September 1987, Mr William Winston and his wife witnessed blood splashing onto the floors of their house and on the walls of several of the rooms. On one grisly occasion, Mrs Winston climbed out of her bath, only to find the floor covered in blood.

Neither she nor her husband were bleeding and to back up this case still further, the blood was analysed and found to be human type O. Mr and Mrs Winston both had type A blood, so where exactly did such gruesome emanations come from?

These poltergeist reports contradict the stereotypical image of what a poltergeist does and what causes it. Poltergeist is German for 'noisy spirit' and they are associated with a range of seemingly inexplicable physical occurrences over a period of time. Such happenings can take the form of strange noises, the movement and destruction of objects, disembodied voices, the appearance of writing on the walls and often, nowadays, the playing of tricks using the telephone, television and other electromagnetic sources. Sometimes, the manifestations can be fairly violent in nature and can last anywhere between a few weeks and a year. Mostly though, they occur in sporadic bursts, seeming to die down, only to reoccur again some time later.

There have been hundreds of cases throughout time, where there have been other occurrences such as inexplicable chills, strange noises, offensive odours and even the levitation of objects, and people have also been linked to poltergeist activity.

The answer to the question 'Where do poltergeists come from?' is a complex one. Many theories have been put forward in an attempt to explain this disturbing phenomenon. Some believe a poltergeist is a spirit trapped between two worlds, while others think the reason behind this comes from the victim's state of mind or emotions. A popular, scientific explanation is that PK (psychokinetic) energy is the cause.

Most people produce this energy naturally and so therefore, in one instance, their 'inner' energy may spill over into the external world, or in another (like that of classic ghost cases) the spirit/entity may 'feed' off this energy. As early as 1930, parapsychologist Hereward Carrington explained the possibility of such energies radiating from the body, especially during puberty. Psychologist Carl Jung also believed this to be the possible cause and he stated that 'When an inner process cannot be integrated, it is often projected outwards'.

It is true that the majority of poltergeist cases have been found to centre on adolescent children. A famous account typical of this is that of the Enfield Poltergeist case. Of all the documented poltergeist incidences, the Enfield outbreak was one of the most dramatic, lasting between August 1977 and September 1978. The Harper family, comprising of four children and their mother, lived in a small house in Enfield, north London, and were said to have been 'driven to distraction' by the longest lasting and the most aggressive outbreak on record. Incidents included the children's beds shaking violently and sounds of shuffling on the carpet (a sound made by someone wearing slippers), often accompanied by the sound of loud knocks. Eventually, *The Daily Mirror* became involved and soon after, The Society for Psychical Research also showed an interest.

In the Enfield case there were many witnesses who, on occasion, described seeing the spirit of a little girl, who had reportedly been suffocated by her father. A medium contacted several entities thought to be responsible for the haunting and later claimed that they were 'feeding' off the negative energy emitted by one of the children – Janet aged eleven. This could have been linked to the children's father leaving a little while before the disturbances began. A record 400 incidents were recorded, some of which were potentially dangerous. Indeed, an iron grille landed near one of the children and the gas fire was torn off the wall. Researchers captured many of the events on film, such as the levitation of two teenage girls in the family and objects, some as large as sofas, being hurled at researchers.

Many apparitions were also sighted, along with the appearance of messages that were left on pieces of paper and even on the walls.

In one particularly frightening instance, Janet began to convulse and went into a trance, during which she produced a drawing of a woman, 'with blood pouring from her throat'.

Underneath it she wrote the word 'Watson'. When tracing back to past occupants of the house, researchers discovered that the Watsons had been the previous tenants and that Mrs Watson had died of throat cancer. On another occasion, one of the other girls started to speak in a gruff voice, claiming it to be that of an old man who had died in the house. The haunting eventually died out during the summer of 1978.

Another case similar to this was that which took place in an apartment in Paris during 1952. The poltergeist activity that took place here centred on the two boys in the Genin family – Henri aged nine and Rene aged thirteen. The phenomenon was witnessed by many different people on several different occasions. In one instance, waiting outside the boys' bedroom, where the activity took place, were some priests, a police officer, a group of scientists, a radio recording team and some psychic investigators with infrared cameras. As midnight struck, they felt a certain 'violence' in the air and watched on in amazement as the boys' furniture began to shake violently.

The dresser banged against the wall and the drawers were flung across the room. A table was moved into the middle of the room and ornaments were thrown, causing deep scoring on the walls.

On another occasion, Rene Genin, whilst in bed, had his pillows snatched from beneath him and he was then lifted and thrown out of bed by a force that was so strong that he was unable to resist it. He was 'terrified' by the experience and the witnesses were equally shocked by what they had just seen. The activity only ever occurred when both boys were present and many photographs were taken, some of which showed a dressing table 'hovering' several inches in the air. A local spiritualist claimed to have made contact with an 'entity' at the time and Catholic priest Father Jean de Freggette witnessed the phenomena and reportedly said, 'One doubts the evidence of one's senses in these matters.' The poltergeist activity lasted for three months, eventually dying out during Christmas of 1952.

According to records dating back several years, it was documented that 'Never before or since have such things been seen by so many independent witnesses and chronicled with such scientific impartiality'. (Source of quote – *Ireland's Own* No. 4,884 July 18th 2003)

The largest ever catalogue of poltergeist activity ever recorded was that which affected a family in Pontefract, West Yorkshire, between August 1966 and the summer of 1969. The activity centred mostly on two of the teenagers in the house: Philip aged fifteen and his sister Diane aged fourteen. Over a hundred different events were noted, some of which were particularly disturbing, such as loud breathing noises, a witness being dragged upstairs by the neck – resulting in marks on her throat – inverted crosses being drawn on the wall, a macabre 'haunting' involving a pair of gloves being made to peer over and underneath doors, witnesses having water, milk and other substances regularly poured over them and green foam emitting from taps when turned on, as well as countless other events that were reported.

There have been suggestions that the identity of the poltergeist may have been a monk – who was hanged for a sex crime some centuries ago – after an apparition of a hooded figure appeared in the house. The house was investigated by many different paranormal researchers at the time and the house was also, according to Colin Wilson – author, critic and philosopher – built on crossed ley lines that enabled such manifestations to occur.

All poltergeists are mischievous, but some can become dangerously violent. One of the notably most violent cases on record took place in Stratford, Connecticut, in 1850. The activity centred on the Phelps family, mostly targeting their children. As well as the usual levitation of objects, noises and apparitions, two of the eldest children were attacked so brutally that when discovered, they were on the brink of death. Luckily, they made a full recovery, although neither of them could remember or explain the attacks.

It is clear from almost all cases that the majority of poltergeist activity is centred on children, especially during puberty; a time of great emotional and physiological stress.

However, it is also true that anyone can fall prey to poltergeist activity. Anyone under huge stress, for example, can trigger off this phenomenon and when the 'victim' seeks help or the negative feelings subside, the poltergeist activity often ceases. Many leading scientists and parapsychologists believe that there is a link between above-average levels of stress, PK events and poltergeist activity. In children, these events are random and undirected, but in an adult, they may be subconsciously directed. A popular theory is that external entities are able to 'latch' on to one particular person, through whom they can use their energy, thereby enabling them to act.

An account of poltergeist phenomenon that does not fall into any of the above categories is that of Greyfriars cemetery in Edinburgh. Its gruesome history includes its use as a mass prison, also being used for witchcraft, body snatching, grave desecration, corpse dumping and live burial. The cemetery's reputation for being haunted is centuries old, but in 1998, something inexplicable began to occur, where visitors encountered cold spots and foul smells and heard loud banging noises. They often found themselves overcome with a sudden feeling of nausea and many were assaulted by an unseen force, resulting in cuts and bruises.

Over a space of two years, an alarming twenty-four people became unconscious whilst in the cemetery and homes nearby also became badly affected. Residents were plagued with such things as objects being levitated, crockery being smashed and the sound of unidentified laughter was also heard on several occasions. There were two failed exorcisms in the area, as well as hundreds of victims and witnesses to the attacks. The entity responsible has been named the 'McKenzie poltergeist'.

Eventually, the attacks became so strong that the section of Greyfriars cemetery that was so badly affected is now chained shut. This extraordinary poltergeist account is one of the best documented and most thoroughly conclusive paranormal cases in history. Never before or since have so many people en masse been affected by such activity, as poltergeist activity usually centres around one individual. This case has baffled scientists all over the world and even sceptics are unable to come up with a rational explanation.

When examining reports of poltergeist phenomena it is important to examine the evidence presented objectively. Old buildings, for example, tend to be noisy at night, when they are 'settling' down and these noises can often be confused with those of a paranormal nature. It can often be difficult to assess photographs and recordings depicting poltergeist activity, because although they may depict objects 'flying' through the air, it does not necessarily show what caused them to fly.

However, this isn't to say that all photographic evidence should be dismissed, for many photographs and video footage show heavy objects and even people levitating, as well as capturing strange, unexplained noises. Indeed, many paranormal investigators have witnessed a variety of poltergeist phenomena and there have been many cases and accounts by reputable witnesses.

Over the last 150 years, the poltergeist phenomenon has been investigated by many scientists, although reports of this trend date back to medieval times. Poltergeist activity is the most frequently reported type of haunting and it is a worldwide phenomenon. In all cases it can be said that poltergeist manifestations are often a way of crying out for attention and so it could therefore be seen as some sort of manifestation of a human spirit that has been driven to extremes when it feels its identity is under threat. However, this does not explain how the poltergeist can 'carry out' such macabre acts as setting fire to things, talking in gruff, disembodied voices or, more sinister, attacking people. It appears that poltergeist activity is usually, but not always, unrelated to hauntings and while hauntings are associated with entities that are deceased, poltergeists can be triggered by a living person's trauma.

5

Natural Causes

Will-o'-the-wisp

Will-o'-the-wisp is a common name for faerie lights. Some legends suggest that will-o'-the-wisp leads people to danger, while others say that if you follow the lights to the end, they will lead you to treasure. Some believe that they are lights carried by elves and that human souls trapped in between earth and the other side follow the lights and ask the elves what will become of them. In England, will-o'-the-wisp is believed to be the souls of boundary movers and swindlers.

The real cause of this 'spooky' phenomenon is phosphorescent flames or lights, often inhabiting swamps, marshes, moors, graveyards or similarly deserted places.

Moisture seems to be a key factor in their sightings and the wisp can be found on land or even at sea. Sailors say they are drowned souls, mourning for their earthly days, and Catholics refer to these sea lights as St Elmo's Fire. This phenomenon is usually seen during autumn and winter months, especially on heavy, overcast days. They are rarely seen on sunny days, as they tend to occur in damp conditions, where the moisture present can be turned into the phosphorous gas.

An example of one of the most popular sightings of this phenomenon is the Marfa lights. These are globes of light that 'hover' around the Mitchell Flats area in Texas. They were first reported by Robert Ellison, a rancher, in 1883. The lights, usually white, red or blue in colour, are described as being about the size of a basketball and 'dancing' above the ground.

They are frequently reported and some believe that the lights are the spirits of the Apache Indians, who once frequented the area.

The dominant explanation is that the lights are a mirage caused by sharp temperature gradients between cold and warm layers of air, thereby allowing moisture to form. Some scientists contend that the lights are the result of a naturally occurring phenomenon – the piezoelectric effect. Discovered by Pierre Curie in 1883, this phenomenon occurs amongst mountainous regions made up of rocks containing quartz that expands during the day and contracts at night. This thermal expansion and contraction creates pressure on the quartz, which is accumulated over time, until it is discharged into the atmosphere, creating the effect of a ball of lightning.

Despite scientific theories, the legend of the Marfa lights has given way to folklore. This shows how easily a phenomenon with a natural cause can evoke people's imaginations and turn them into a mass hysteria.

St Elmo's Fire:

A luminous glow can often be seen at night from the tops of ships' masts, hovering above cattle or, in some cases, above people. This ghostly apparition is known as St Elmo's fire – named after Saint Elmo, the patron saint of sailors. It has, in the past, been wrongly reported as a ball of lightning; however, it is, in fact, a corona discharge that produces plasma.

The electric field around the object in question causes ionisation of the air molecules, thereby producing a vivid glow that is visible in low light conditions. The 'flames' may be many inches long and are often accompanied by audible crackling noises.

Accounts of this phenomenon vary widely, although most reports mention one or more of the following characteristics: a spherical 'fireball' of between half an inch (1 cm) and 6-and-a-half feet (2 m), often occurring just before or during a thunderstorm; a white-, red-, yellow- or blue-coloured flame hovering just above the ground lasting for several seconds, often accompanied by an explosion or 'popping' sound and a sulphurous smell; and there is a tendency for the fireball to hover over conducting paths of electricity, such as telegraph wires and pylons. They have also been known to enter houses through chimneys and to leave underneath doors.

A fascinating report of St Elmo's fire entering a building was that which entered a house in Miami, Florida. The description given was similar to many ghost light and ball lightning reports, but in some ways, this one is a little more unusual. The ball of light had entered via the window and had moved towards the witness, forcing him to the ground. It had then exited through the hall window and although both windows were screened, there was no damage to either. The witness' wife had also seen small balls of fire, of about 6 to 8 inches in diameter, moving through the window quite some time before her husband had noticed the larger ball of light.

Another family from Fleetwood, Lancashire, also experienced this strange phenomenon during the early part of the evening of 3 December 1979. They described a ghost light, possibly ball lightning, of about 6 inches in diameter, that floated down the chimney, which was sealed, and it then moved into their living room. They reportedly said, 'It was a purple colour, transparent, but appeared to have a fiery glow surrounding it. It eventually disappeared with a loud crack, leaving behind a sulphurous smell.'

6

Manifestations Of Energy

Orbs:

The term orb is the name given to spherical light anomalies that have often shown up in photographs, appearing mostly when people do not expect it. A popular leading theory concerning what orbs are is that they are not actual spirits, but more so the energy that is transferred from a source, such as power lines, heat energy and people, as the actual spirit needs to gain energy in order to manifest itself. This may not be a conscious thing the spirit is doing, but simply a natural way of obtaining energy. This would explain why orbs appear as round balls, as according to the laws of physics, energy transfers assume the natural shape of a sphere.

Orbs sometimes appear when a spirit presence is nearby and they can either be completely transparent, white and glowing, or in a solid black form. Small orbs use up less energy in manifesting themselves than apparitions do and during the colder months of the year, ghosts find it easier to appear as a full apparition, appearing as they were when alive, owing to the level of static electricity in the atmosphere. Orbs tend to surround people, as they draw energy when needed, and as the orb gains more energy, it tends to enlarge; when enough energy is gained, the spirit may then be able to manifest itself.

When examining the appearance of orbs in photographs, it is important to assess whether it could be reflections from dust particles, insects or moisture droplets on the camera lens.

When all of these are accounted for, what you are left with could be an example of genuine spirit orbs.

Vortices:

In paranormal terms, a vortex is a manifestation of energy associated with ghosts and spirits. There have been many different theories and ideas about what a vortex actually is. A popular theory is that it is a spirit's energy, much like that of an orb, and yet it is said to signify a stronger paranormal presence.

Most, if not all, parapsychologists and paranormal investigators agree that a vortex is a gateway through which entities may pass. Usually, it assumes a funnel-like shape or a cylindrical form. Another possible theory explaining the appearance of vortices is that they could easily be mistaken for an orb in motion, which can often appear as a white contrail that bends in different directions.

It is, however, said to be very unusual to capture a vortex on camera and film, although some researchers such as paranormal investigator Robert Appleton have seemingly captured many on camera.

7

Celestial Phenomena Supernatural Beings or Hallucinations?

Demons:

The term 'demon' is derived from the Greek word *daimon* or, alternatively, *daemon*. It was once used to describe all supernatural beings – good and bad; however, Christians branded all pagan spirits as Satanic. Demons have never had a human form; indeed, their frightening, evil appearance is said to mirror that of their master – Satan.

Occultists have claimed to be able to conjure up demons from the underworld using magical spells, whilst protecting themselves in a magic circle. Necromancy, as it is called, originated with the Mesopotamians thousands of years ago and is still practised today. Not all demons, however, arrive on the Earthly plane by invitation; there are accounts of such entities having arrived of their own free will.

The idea of demons is not popular with parapsychologists.

Instead, they prefer a more scientific approach, with a credible hypothesis. Some, however, believe that demons could be objective entities that feed on negative, emotional energy that has been released by mankind, thus allowing them through the veil and to manifest in our world.

Incubi and succubi:

A common form of demon is the incubus, said to be a male demon that preys on sleeping females, often having intercourse with the woman, while her partner remains in an unnaturally deep sleep beside her. Victims who report suffering from this phenomenon describe feeling pressure on the bed, on their chest or on other parts of the body. Some even describe being strangled as part of their experience.

Incubi are said to feed on psychic energy, which they need in order to manifest, and many victims describe feeling 'exhausted' after their experience.

Succubus is the female form of the incubus. This demon preys on sleeping men, much like how its partner the incubus preys on women. However, unlike the incubi, this demon tends to choose single men and embodies itself as their ex-partners.

The victim may not even see the entity and yet they may feel its presence.

Scientific explanations state that the incubus is nothing more than sleep paralysis, which produces effects similar to those described by the 'victims' – that they are merely in a state between the unconscious and the conscious and so therefore hypnagogic and hypnopompic hallucinations occur. Sleep paralysis is a condition where the individual, often on the brink of sleep, realises that they are unable to move or speak. This sensation can last from anything from a few seconds to several minutes. An accompanying malevolent presence is often felt with this sensation and a sense of 'dread' is also very common.

The waking brain tries to find an explanation for the experience and it therefore 'invents' the evil entity.

Investigations show that forty per cent of the population has had this experience at least once; however, the sleep-paralysis theory does not explain the sexual attacks that are so often reported with these cases. There are many who believe the entities are very real and some victims claim it has happened to them while they have been fully awake. Sceptics claim that reports of incubi and succubi show signs of sexual frustration, while psychologists believe there could be a link between sexual abuse and the incubus phenomenon, but, as yet, nothing has been proven.

Angels:

The term 'angel' comes from the Latin *angelos* and they are said to be messengers of God and there have been many reports and sightings of guardian angels appearing during times of crisis. There have also been instances of angels appearing on the front line during the First World War.

Legend has it that in August 1914, thousands of soldiers saw an angel in the sky during the bloody battle of Mons. Some years later, researchers and scientists claimed that the intense hunger of these soldiers, coupled with the awful conditions at that time, caused the soldiers to experience mass hallucinations. The Angel of Mons story shows just how myth and reality can be mixed up to a point where it is hard to distinguish fact from fiction.

Stories of unexplained rescues by spirit beings that appear in times of need have been well documented throughout recorded history. In one such case, it is reported by the paediatric professor Dr Frank Oski that one night he went to bed thinking about one of his dying patients, but he felt powerless to help and subsequently went to sleep wondering why it was that the child had to die. About an hour after falling asleep, Oski was awakened by a bright light that had entered his room. He could make out the form of a female with wings in the glow, who was approximately 20 years of age. In a quiet, reassuring tone, the woman began to explain to the speechless Dr Oski why it was that children had to die.

He recalls the angel saying, 'Life is an endless cycle of improvements and humans are not perfect yet. Most people have this secret revealed to them when they die, but handicapped children often know this and endure their problems without complaining, because they know their burdens will pass.' Oski spoke freely of his experience and later wrote about it in a paediatric journal.

Sceptics have dismissed reports such as this, claiming that the brain produces such hallucinations as a way of coping with a negative situation. However, it is important to keep an open mind on the many reports of sightings of angels that continue to occur around the world on a daily basis.

8

Imaginary or Mystical Beings

Fairies:

On the subject of folklore, for many centuries now, fairies have caused much debate as to whether or not they actually exist. It seems that some people are willing to believe in the existence of fairies or the 'little people' that often appear in children's stories. Often, these are bound up with happy memories of childhood and are recalled with delight, yet for most people, they stand as a lost illusion and few believe in their actual existence.

In the Far East, the belief in fairies is strong and many who live there have claimed to have seen fairies on several occasions. Research studies suggest that it is more common for children to see them, perhaps due to their innocence and purity. The most famous case involving fairy 'photographs' was the Cottingley case. In 1917, two girls, 16-year-old Elsie Wright and her 10-year-old cousin Francis Griffiths, claimed to have captured fairies on camera whilst playing in Cottingley Glen.

Upon examining the photos, they were found to be fakes, simply produced by the girls cutting out pictures of fairies and posing next to them. There have, in fact, been no documented photographs/evidence depicting 'real' fairies.

The question posed by most researchers is: Why do most people not see fairies? Believers in fairies claim that the reason for this is that their bodies are less dense than ours, making them appear translucent. A special sense such as ESP (extrasensory perception) must be awakened in people if they are to see fairies, as the world in which fairies live does not affect our ordinary senses directly. They cannot be touched, yet they can certainly be seen, owing to the 'light' they give off. A strong reason for the majority of people being unable to see them is because of a difference in perspective, although whether a strong belief in fairies can make them manifest is yet another topic open to debate.

Djinns:

In Arabian and Muslim folklore, djinns are ugly, evil demons that have supernatural powers. The name comes from an Arabic word meaning 'to hide' or 'conceal'. In the Western world, they are called genies, and the highest of the djinns is the Devil. The djinns were thought by some in Islamic culture to be spirits that were lower than angels, because they are made up of fire and because they are not immortal. They can take on both human and animal shapes in order to influence man to do good or evil.

In Islamic lore, the djinns were an intermediate creation, coming between humankind and angels. King Solomon, the son of David, was the King of Israel in the tenth century BC. He was said to have tamed numerous djinns and to have become their leader, with the help of his magic ring. He allegedly ordered them to build the temple at Jerusalem, as well as beautiful gardens and palaces.

In The Arabian Nights, djinns or genies came from Aladdin's lamp. However, there are several myths concerning the home of the djinns. Some say they lived and roamed in the desert, while others believe they existed in the mountains, along with other supernatural beings. Believers of the djinn state that they are real entities living on Earth, which are usually invisible to humans. Like fairies, scientists claim they do not exist and that they simply play a role in mythology. Many psychologists state that as with many other 'folklore' stories, tales of djinns are passed down from one generation to another. As the origins of these stories come from religious cultures, where depictions of good and evil play such integral roles, there is already a justification to create such entities in the mind.

9

Past Lives

Reincarnation is based upon the Buddhist idea of 'karma'. It is a measure of a person's good and bad deeds in life that determines their position in their new Earth body. Past life regression has been proved by psychologists to be particularly helpful in assessing a 'past life' case. For example, a person suffering from a phobia would be put into a hypnotic state and regressed back to another lifetime. It often transpires that a certain incident, possibly linked to their death in a previous existence, is the source of the phobia shown in their current personality.

In one case, a patient studied by Californian psychologist Dr Edith Fiore complained of terrible head pains and was 'terrified of the colour red'. During regression, she described witnessing her own murder – she had been 'hit over the head with a club and blood was spurting everywhere'.

There are other cases of consciously recalled past lives, such as those that emerge in very young children, and past lives as the opposite sex are not uncommon, although the divide appears less than fifty/fifty. Under hypnosis, it usually emerges that the patient suffered a poverty-stricken past or a violent death in their previous life. Although there have been several cases of past lives, some scientists claim that there are several explanations that may account for memory of a past life.

Multiple personality disorder:

It has been suggested that perhaps, whilst under hypnosis, a patient can somehow tap into their inner psyche, revealing characteristic personality traits that could possibly have been missing from their own persona.

45

For example, a cowardly person may have inner strength or courage hidden deep down within their own personality. This may emerge during regression.

Genetic memory:

This suggestion puts forwards the idea that just as genes pass on both behavioural and physical characteristics from parent to child, so, too, can memories be transferred down the chain. This, however, is not a stable theory, as no memory of events after the birth of a child have ever been recalled – indeed, it is mostly only death scenes – therefore death must post-date the birth of an ancestor, meaning that the memory could not be passed on.

There are also a considerable amount of cases involving recollections of childless past lives, for if there are no children, the genes cannot be passed on.

Clairvoyance:

Some believe it could be possible to gather information from a deceased personality like a clairvoyant, without necessarily being aware of this fact. However, recollections of past lives never feature 'messages' that could possibly have been given by the deceased person – only descriptions of the trivia in their life have been noted.

Collective Unconscious:

The idea of analytical psychology was developed by Swiss psychologist Carl Jung. He believed that all mental activity enters a collective pool and we are all part of this pool; therefore, we are able to 'tap' into it at any given time in order to produce past lives. Jung distinguished the collective unconscious from the personal unconscious. Along with Sigmund Freud, Jung pioneered theories of the relationships between the conscious and the unconscious aspects of the mind.

Jung perceived the primary motivating force to be spiritual in origin. According to Jung, psychic phenomena such as precognition, telepathy and synchronicity were all manifestations of the collective unconscious. This theory, however, fails to explain why different past lives are never recalled by a patient.

The Hindu tradition of the 'Akashic Record', which stores everything everybody has ever done, can, it is said, be obtained through deep meditation. Another theory has been suggested by biologist Dr Rupert Sheldrake, in which he explains how all life forms are moulded by a morphic resonance or energy field – a theory that many other scientists tend to favour. Habits and personality traits are then passed on in an unseen and universal 'consciousness', thus shaping the template of this life field using 'individual contributions' from each living entity.

Therefore, it could be a possibility that human beings are a consciousness within a far greater consciousness, with traits of earlier humans being found within our 'selves'.

Overall, there appear to be three main viewpoints that offer different evaluations on the phenomenon of past lives.

They are as follows:

Scientific – this explanation is that energy cannot be destroyed, so therefore it must jump from one energy source to another. This could explain how the energy of our mind or spirit would continue to exist in different forms.

Philosophical – this system has a great deal to offer on the concept of life after death. Like the scientific school of thought, reincarnation is thought to be based on energy, however, philosophers state that this is a direct influence from the surrounding cosmos. Similarities are shown with rebirth and the falling of rain, i.e. all life cycles.

Spiritual – spiritualists take on the stance of posing questions such as, 'If everybody that is born has a new soul, wouldn't heaven be overcrowded by now?' Therefore, there must be some kind of turnaround, where past lives would offer a solution to this problem. The idea of past lives transforms any examination of spiritual questions.

The main problem of assessing the validity of past-life experiences is as a result of the fact that much of the evidence emerges from hypnotised subjects. Hypnosis is an altered state of consciousness, in which the subject becomes susceptible to influence. The subject, in turn, feels the need to please the hypnotist. The hypnotic state enhances memory and fantasy equally, which consequently creates unreliable accounts.

However, not all past-life memories emerge through hypnosis. Children have been known to recall past memories from previous existences, often to the amazement of their parents. Often, obscure details emerge which, after rigorously checking, may well prove to be accurate.

Whatever the explanation, one fact still remains – more and more cases of individuals' accounts of their past lives are being documented and many researchers and scientists still show an active interest in such studies.

10

Contacting the Dead

For centuries, many different methods have been used to make contact with the deceased. Some of these practices can be dangerous to novices, without the aid of a trained medium, and they should never be undertaken lightly.

Spiritualism And Mediumship:

Spiritualism is a movement involving psychic communicators, who believe they can contact the deceased. Many of the spirits they claim to make contact with have not been able to make it to 'the other side' and therefore they exist on planes between worlds, making it easier for them to communicate with the 'living' world.

Spiritualism has existed for centuries and has been (and still is) practised in many different cultures by shamans and seers, as well as mediums. The modern spiritualist movement, however, began in 1848. In December 1847, Methodist farmer John Fox, his wife and two daughters, Margaret aged fourteen and Kate aged twelve, moved into a small house in Hydesville, New York. Not long after they had moved in the family began to hear loud banging and rapping noises. This went on for some time and eventually, the spirit identified itself as a pedlar named Charles B. Rosna, who had been murdered in the house by a blacksmith called John C. Bell. That summer, the Foxes followed the spirit's directions to dig up the cellar and in doing so, they discovered a human skeleton. Some fifty years later, more bones were discovered, along with a pedlar's tin.

Following this event, public interest escalated and the girls, who claimed to be able to make contact with the spirit, were encouraged to hold a seance. In 1851, however, three professors from Buffalo

49

University, New York, claimed that whilst investigating the Fox sisters, they found that fraudulent methods had been used to create the rapping sounds, although this did not stop the development of spiritualism and by this time, many groups and churches had already started to do so.

Interest in spiritualism peaked between 1850 and 1890 and throughout these years, claims of phenomena witnessed at seances included full spirit materialisation and levitation of mediums. However, The Society for Psychical Research (SPR) began to impose strict test conditions on mediums and as a result, such marvels diminished and then subsequently ceased completely. There is a strong reason to believe that almost every professional Victorian medium practised fraud at some point or other.

During the late 1800s, a Mrs Samuel Guppy became one of London's most prominent mediums. Born under the name of Agnes Nichol, her mediumistic powers were first discovered in 1866. A year later, she married Samuel Guppy and shortly after, she became renowned for her seances that included table movements, rappings, levitations and emanations such as lobsters, live eels and butterflies. In spite of her success, Mrs Guppy was highly jealous of another medium called Florence Cook and the pair continued to engage in a bitter feud throughout their careers and this bitter rivalry led to Mrs Guppy sabotaging Florence Cook's seances on more than one occasion.

Spiritualism is not merely a way in which psychically gifted people can contact the dead, but it also embraces other paranormal activity, such as telekinesis – the ability to influence matter or energy to move objects, without the use of physical means – ectoplasm, which can take on the human form, and direct voice mediums. The latter involves the spirit directly speaking through the mouth of the medium, whilst they are in a trance-like state. Most mediums have a spirit guide who protects them and who often helps to give information to the medium by communicating with the spirit.

Mediums are generally split into two types: mental and physical. Mental mediums use ESP (extrasensory perception), which enables spirit communications to take place. Spirit voices are then 'heard' and can take on forms such as automatic writing and drawing. Physical mediumship is where the medium acts as a 'channel' for psychokinetic (PK) effects initiated by the deceased. These can take on forms such as the levitation of objects and people, and even the spirit manifesting itself in a substance called ectoplasm, which extrudes from the orifices of the medium's body. Ectoplasm is a strange, luminous substance that is cold to the touch and is said to have the same texture as paste, or, in some cases, liquid.

There are many witnesses and photographs of mediums producing this substance, but their authenticity has yet to be proved.

Spiritualism has confronted the world of science and many mediums have been rigorously tested. Throughout recent years, enough positive results have been achieved to convince many scientists of its authenticity; however, this is not to say that there are no 'fakes' in existence, as many 'so-called' mediums have been uncovered as fraudsters.

Parapsychologists often work alongside mediums and parapsychology dates back over a hundred years and involves the study of mental phenomena outside the sphere of ordinary psychology, i.e. hypnosis, telepathy and the scientific testing of mediumship. It is the parapsychologist's job to investigate individuals who claim to possess mediumistic abilities that allow them to contact the 'spirit world'. They are interested in such studies because, if valid, they could provide evidence to support the survival of bodily death. Neuropsychological research challenges as to whether personality and consciousness is dependent on a living brain and it also questions whether or not the mind is, in fact, separate from the brain – an aspect of psychology which was also explored by Carl Jung.

Parapsychologists use EMF (electromagnetic field) meters to measure fluctuations in energy to establish whether or not a paranormal phenomenon is taking place. Some mediums question the reliability of using such equipment, as it does not always give an accurate reading. Electrical equipment in the building, power stations, nearby railway lines, subtle magnetic shifts in the earth's atmosphere and even storms can all affect the reading, causing a certain degree of inaccuracy.

Seances:

As old as spiritualism itself, seances have been used for many years as a way in which to contact the dead. A seance involves a number of people wishing to make contact with their loved ones or even with a spirit responsible for 'haunting' their homes. All those present are usually seated around a table, often with a medium present. The medium begins by opening the seance, asking for protection from their spirit guides, and this is followed by a prayer. They then continue by asking if any spirit is present, often being answered with a series of rapping noises.

During a seance, paranormal activity of some kind is often experienced. Scientists and non-believers discredit this though, as they state that the main cause for 'paranormal events' taking place is a combination of mass hysteria, a build up of PK energy from the people present and even simply someone present who 'cheats'. However, those who have attended seances claim that what they have experienced cannot be explained by scientific theories alone. Many have been witness to events such as vases and crockery levitating, flying across the room and then smashing. Others claim to have experienced more subtle signs of a presence, such as an unfamiliar aroma or 'cold spots' in the room.

Occasionally, with the presence of a medium, communication with the deceased can take place. Sometimes, however, if attempted within a person's home, such contact can often make matters worse and the 'haunting' can increase, perhaps even becoming more aggressive. There is also a danger that evil spirits posing as 'loved ones' can use the seance to travel into the living world. This is especially dangerous if there is no medium present to 'close down' the seance.

The Ouija Board:

Ouija boards, believe it or not, were once found in toy stores across America and even today, in some states, they are still sold as a 'board game'. 'Ouija' is a combination of the French word *oui* and German *ja*, both meaning yes. It is a board marked with letters of the alphabet as well as various other signs and it is used in conjunction with a movable pointer, often a glass or planchette, which the participants place their fingers on to facilitate the obtaining of messages from the spirit world. Planchettes are often used on their own with a pencil, in order to attain so-called automatic writing. It is believed that the board has no power in itself, but is used rather as a tool to aid a medium while in communication with the spirit world.

It is imperative that unless a trained medium is present, you should never attempt to invoke spirits by using an ouija board or similar device.

This is because only a medium has the ability to safely open and close down the 'seance' and only a medium has protection from their spirit guide. Without this, the seance will remain open, allowing nasty spirits to enter whenever they choose to. The easiest way to understand this is to imagine a curtain or veil, which exists between our world and that of the spirit. This curtain, once opened, allows any spirit who so desires to make contact to enter. If it is not closed, they will carry on coming through and once in, they can be difficult to remove. Some practitioners claim to have had bad experiences related to the use of ouija boards and they claim to be 'haunted' by 'demons' as a result.

A few paranormal researchers claim that the majority of 'demonic possession' cases are caused by the use of ouija boards. Indeed, evil spirits will often disguise themselves as loved ones and perhaps even take over that person's life.

Research by occultist Manly Palmer Hall suggests that 'Out of every hundred such cases, at least ninety-five are worse off for the experience'. There is much debate within religious ideology, as Christians and Roman Catholic priests believe that ouija boards are dangerous and that by using these devices, a person opens themselves to demonic possession.

Electronic Voice Phenomena (EVP):

This is a form of spiritual communication and it concerns unexpected voices being found in recording media or through other electronic audio devices. Instrumental Trans Communication (ITC) is a modern term that includes all of the ways these unexpected voices and images are collected.

EVP was not defined until the mid-twentieth century, although it is reported to have taken place in various forms since the earlier part of the century. The origins of EVP began with Attila Von Szalay, a photographer and medium, who claimed that he tape-recorded voices of the dead during the 1930s. Later, in the 1950s, he joined up with paranormal researcher Raymond Bayless and together, they began experimenting using a 78-rpm Pack-Bell record cutter. The results from using this equipment remained inconclusive, so they later moved on to make a custom-made recording rig featuring a microphone inside a soundproofed closet. Using this set-up, Szalay and Bayless claim to have captured unexplained auditory phenomena, which was later published in the *Journal of The American Society for Psychical Research.*

The most famous account of EVP is generally said to be when Swedish researcher Friedrich Jürgenson captured the voice of his dead mother in 1958, whilst recording birdsong in a Norwegian wood. Soon to follow Jürgenson was Dr Konstantin Raudive, a Latvian, who invented a new method for producing EVP. Raudive was an excellent publicist and soon, the phenomenon was named 'Raudive Voices'. This was unfair to Jürgenson and so the publisher Colin Smythe invented the term 'Electronic Voice Phenomena'.

In around 1982, there were a number of significant developments in EVP. Indeed, in America, a system named 'Spiricom' was widely publicised. The idea behind the machine was to allow conversations between the living and the dead to take place. The machine used radio frequencies that changed when a spirit attempted some form of communication, allowing the spirit to superimpose a message on the background noise. Some of the recordings were very clear and many parapsychologists stated that either the messages were, indeed, proof of contact with the dead, or that they were an outright hoax. However, until the experiments are duplicated by scientists, this work will never be accepted as proof in itself.

In the 1990s, a new and successful system called the EVP maker was invented by Stefan Bion in Germany, which proved to be more accurate and which produced high-quality speech/EVP in abundance. More recently, in 2003, writer David Ellis conducted an experiment at The Institute of Noetic Sciences (IONS), California – a research organisation founded by Apollo astronaut Captain Ed Mitchell. The experiment proved to be a huge success, with several voices being recorded and a report on the experiment was published by The Society for Psychical Research.

Supposedly, a haunted aircraft – the Romeo Foxtrot 398 – has also been the subject of similar experiments. Indeed, one worker allegedly saw a ghost on board one night and so a group was formed. Their experiment involved leaving several cameras and two tape recorders running on the locked aircraft.

They promptly left the scene and upon returning quite some time later, they found one of the cameras to be opened.

They listened to the tape recordings and were astonished to hear faint noises of Morse code blips, voices and hangar doors opening and closing. Were these recordings proof of survival?

Or could there be a more plausible explanation?

Chingle Hall is also another location where EVP has been recorded. Here, tape recordings captured a series of loud knocks and footsteps in the 'priest's room', whilst visual images were also captured on camera in one of the bedrooms. EVP still continues today, although technology has come a long way since the days of Bayless and Von Szalay's custom-made recording rig. Recently, many who use EVP recording equipment claim that they have received predictions warning them of catastrophic events, such as Hurricane Katrina that hit New Orleans in 2005. The credibility of these reports has yet to be proven and there is still much debate surrounding EVP.

Sceptics claim that there could be a variety of rational explanations for such phenomena, with interference being the most likely, as certain instances of EVP represent radio signals of voices/sounds from broadcast sources. Some sceptics have also suggested that many alleged examples of EVP may not be voices at all, but, instead, are the result of pareidolia – a condition created when the brain incorrectly interprets random patterns as being familiar patterns. In the case of EVP, the interpretation of random noise stimuli is mistaken for the familiar sound of a human voice.

A number of explanations have been put forward by the paranormal community. Some believe that EVP is caused by psychokinesis created by the researcher's subconscious ability to influence energy matter without physical means and they claim that all living human beings are capable of producing EVP. EVP has not been accepted by mainstream science; however, paranormal investigators support this phenomenon as proof for survival.

11

Out-of-Body Experiences

Out-of-body experiences (or OOBEs for short) are a much studied and researched phenomenon. There is vast progress in afterlife research in this field and a growing number of scientists, neurologists and physicists share the theory that the brain is not the origin of consciousness and that the mind is separate, existing as an electromagnetic field around the body.

There have been many documented cases of OOBEs and a few people claim to have the ability to induce them at will.

Descriptions of OOBEs seem to bear an interesting resemblance to the phases that deceased spirits are said to pass through after death.

Robert Monroe, an American researcher of out-of-body experiences, believes that we all experience OOBEs during our sleep without realising it. He has written many books about his own experiences and says, 'Dreams of flying are a rationalisation of what an out-of-body experience is ... A falling dream is the re-entering of the physical body.' There are reports of experiences of lucid dreams or flying dreams that exhibit many of the attributes associated with the OOBE.

Psychologists have many different perspectives and theories on the subject. Dr Susan Blackmore is one of the world's leading researchers of the OOBE and she works from the objective approach and claims to have had an out-of-body experience herself. In her research studies, Blackmore compared four different surveys, showing that almost 800 people claimed to have experienced an OOBE. This research suggests that 18 per cent of the population believe that they have had an out-of-body experience at some point in their lives. Many described 'being near the ceiling looking down on themselves', as well as a feeling of 'flying through the air'. Such experiences are akin to those of the near-death experience or NDE.

The term 'near-death experience', or NDE, was coined by American medic Dr Raymond Moody, in his ground-breaking book *Life After Life*, published in November 1975. Scientific examination of the NDE phenomenon presents persuasive evidence to suggest that the mind and body are separate entities; therefore, the mind can survive the demise of the physical body. Near-death experiences have long been at the centre of medical controversy. Unlike the OOBE, which is experienced whilst asleep, the NDE occurs when a person enters into death. Often, whilst on the operating table, patients have described a sense of floating above their own body, or seeing a bright light at the end of a tunnel.

Experimental data suggests that the most common feature of an OOBE or NDE is the person observing themselves from a position above the body. It is argued that this could not be possible, as their 'self' does not have eyes in which to see themselves. However, it is worth considering the findings of psychology professor Dr Kenneth Ring and his colleague Sharon Cooper, in which they interviewed thirty blind people, who had all undergone near-death experiences, and they discovered that several were able to accurately describe their resuscitation room.

From 1977, Dr Ring has contributed greatly to the scientific research of NDEs. In 1980, the professor published the results of his studies – *Life at Death: A Scientific Investigation of the Near-Death Experience* – and his system of questioning has since been used as the standard method for interviewing NDE subjects. Later on, in 1992, Dr Ring published the results of an in-depth research experiment, in which he studied the psychological profiles of those who had experienced the NDE phenomenon, and he was able to show that religious background, race and age had no bearing on the experience.

In 1982, George Gallup Jr. of the famous international Gallup Organization found that eight million Americans had experienced an NDE. This ground-breaking research showed that the phenomenon was more prevalent than had previously been thought. Gallup's results are regarded as being the most accurate data so far. It was, however, Dr Raymond Moody who identified the main components of the NDE. They are as follows:

A sense of being dead – in which subjects are initially unaware that they are, in fact, 'dead'. They find themselves floating above the body, looking down on themselves. When they eventually recognise the body as being their own, they begin to experience fear, followed by an understanding and an awareness of what is going on around them. If they are successfully resuscitated, they can recall exact details of medical procedures and other observations.

Peace and painlessness – in which before the experience, people are often in severe discomfort. However, once they are released from the body, all pain is left behind and a sense of spiritual peace pervades.

The out-of-body experience – this can occur away from life-threatening situations. However, at the point when the subject is pronounced dead, they will become aware that they are now a separate entity from the body. Whilst in this out-of-body state, the subject can observe things that are happening elsewhere.

The tunnel journey – this is where once the subject accepts their death, far from feeling sadness, they are filled with a sense of exhilaration. They now enter a dark tunnel, at the end of which is a bright light. Occasionally, the subject is accompanied by a being, said to be an angel, who guides them towards the light.

Other-world beings – this is the belief that at the end of the tunnel lies a place that is described as being engulfed in bright light, a beautiful garden or the gateway to heaven itself and it is here that there are other beings that glow intensely. The subject feels pure love and deceased relatives and friends greet them in this place.

The ultimate being of light – is where the subject becomes aware of a supreme being of light, with whom people of a religious background can identify as being God, Jesus, Allah or Buddha. The being radiates such love and understanding that when the subject is told it is time to return, as it is not yet their 'time', they do not want to leave.

The life review – is where before returning to their earthly body, the subject is often confronted by a life review. The entire person's life is presented before them: every act, good and bad.

The subject then feels the emotions they have generated in others. The life review can also be experienced by a person on the point of death, without experiencing a 'full' NDE. Often, people have stated that, 'My whole life passed in front of me'.

During an NDE, time does not pass in the same way as it normally does; instead, it is greatly compressed.

The return from death – is where many people do not want to return to their physical bodies and the return journey is usually much quicker than the journey out. Subjects often re-enter the body head first, at the speed of a bullet.

Aftermath of the near-death experience – this NDE experience can totally change the outlook of an individual, sometimes even making a person more spiritual. Many see the irrelevancies of organised religion and come away with a positive outlook on life, without fear of death. The subject feels that there are now only two things which are important: knowledge and love. Some people go on to develop psychic or clairvoyant powers.

Many researchers are beginning to look to 'ancient wisdom' for the answer and it seems that in *The Tibetan Book of the Dead*, composed by many seers including the Dalai Lama, such experiences were predicted thirteen centuries ago. The teachings of the great Buddhist master Padmasambhava in the eighth century state that, 'Even though you may have been blind, deaf or lame while you were alive, now your eyes see forms, your ears hear sounds and all your sense faculties are faultless, clear and complete.' It seems, therefore, that ancient civilisations agree that NDEs do exist.

NDEs have been reported by historical figures such as Plato, Bede and Tolstoy, and yet it is, however, only in the last thirty years that medical science has turned its attention to the phenomenon. There are more cases of people claiming to have 'come back' after dying than ever before and for many who have experienced an NDE, their adventures seem to provide evidence for life after death. Many scientists, however, claim that these 'experiences' are merely hallucinations produced by the dying brain.

A popular theory associates the NDE with the experiences of birth and that the OOBE is simply reliving this moment. The tunnel in which the spirit travels down is the birth canal and the 'white light' is the light of the world into which we are born. This theory was proposed by Stanislav Grof and Joan Halifax in 1977 and later popularised by astronomer Carl Sagan. However, it is inadequate as a satisfactory explanation for NDEs. The newborn infant would not be able to 'see' the birth canal whilst being born, as its eyes are closed, and at that stage it would not have the mental skills or capacity to recognise its surroundings. Therefore, it would be impossible for an adult to reconstruct what it was like to be an infant.

There are a number of scientists, who continue to disregard OOBEs. They state that those who claimed to have had an OOBE said that they 'saw' things during the experience and these details were later checked and found to be incorrect.

Some psychologists believe that certain psychological conditions, such as stress, may cause a feeling of 'depersonalisation' or a sensation of being out of the body and scientists argue that the best way to understand such experiences is by looking at neurochemistry, physiology and psychology, as these perspectives question the nature of consciousness.

So are NDEs the prelude to life after death, or the very last experience we have before dying? Theories in modern physics claim that all physical objects may be based on underlying fields of particle energies that can appear, disappear and relocate themselves randomly. Just as cycles of the seasons are a consequence of a turning world, life and death are seen as two inseparable facets of continuity. Some physicists argue that the mind is timeless and spaceless – as the OOBE implies – and therefore consciousness may be eternal and could be seen to survive death.

12

Mysterious Objects and Extraterrestrial Beings

UFOs:

UFO sightings are not a recent phenomenon. There have been millions of reported sightings from almost every country in the world and one of the earliest was from Switzerland. On 7 August 1566, strange lights were regularly seen in the sky and there are many illustrations showing this. Nobody really knew or understood what they were; however, we now simply know them as UFOs.

This account, however, was not the earliest. Indeed, far earlier, sightings have been described in the Bible – in Ezekiel, chapter 1, the prophet writes of a 'whirlwind' and a manifestation of 'a wheel in the middle of a wheel' that 'fired lightning bolts to the Earth'. Was this a description of a UFO?

Most people imagine a UFO as being a saucer-shaped object. This is true for some accounts; however, many sightings describe other shapes, such as cylinders, rows of lights and triangles. Many witnesses have taken photographs of UFOs, some of which have been closely examined, and as no other explanation can be given, these photographs are said to be true encounters of UFOs. There is a huge variety of UFOs, which can be found in almost every paranormal book or website; however, many have been proven to be fakes and unfortunately, these make up the vast majority of UFO photographs.

As well as reported sightings of UFOs, many have claimed that they have even been abducted. There are reports of people having been out driving in their cars, when they have 'seen' bright lights and heard a 'strange hovering sound', after which they cannot recall what happens immediately following this experience. Often, they find themselves waking in their car, only to find they have lost four or five hours of their time. Later, as their memories return, they tell of terrifying ordeals of abduction and alien experiments; some even discover mysterious marks on their body.

In March 2000, a series of UFO incidents hit Lincolnshire, including two cases of human interaction and several UFO sightings. A local fruit vendor Tony Kirby observed a white 'unearthly-looking' object hovering in the sky. The RAF claimed they had no aircraft in the area at the time and there were many other similar sightings that took place in the area, around the same time, by different witnesses.

At the beginning of April 2000, 68-year-old Cliff Blyth told the local newspaper that he had been hit by a 2 inch (5 cm) red ball of fire that shot through a closed window and into his chest. His wife had witnessed the experience; however, no marks could be found on his body and he suffered no physiological effects after the incident. About the same time, another witness reported seeing a bright red light travelling through the sky.

There are six common types of UFO, as listed below:

The amber gambler – this is a small ball of light, slightly larger than a star, that is usually orange, yellow or red in colour. It moves quickly and is often only seen for a few minutes. Attracted to power lines, it is the most popular type of UFO and is responsible for 22 per cent of UFO cases.

The cigar tube – this is a long, cigar-like object that is common in the daytime and silver in colour. It is more likely to be seen in random places, it does not affect people or vehicles and it makes up 16 per cent of UFO sightings.

The flying football – this is an oval-shaped object that can be seen day or night. It is mostly white, but it can also be red or yellow; some can also be purple in colour, which suggests UV rays. They are mostly seen around motor vehicles, out of windows, and are attracted to metal. Power stations, bridges and roads are the most popular places for it to manifest and it is responsible for 14 per cent of cases.

The Saturn shape – resembling the planet Saturn (hence the name), it is a common daylight type of UFO and is metallic in appearance. Seen nearer to ground level, this UFO often interferes with people and vehicles, involving people claiming abduction. Hovering and rotating, it can be seen near water and is responsible for 11 per cent of cases.

The saucer – resembling a large, upturned dish, many have lights inset in the base and it is generally seen in the daytime. Common in North and South America, this type of UFO has also appeared over the Pennines in England and there have been reported sightings from forty years ago, although they are not so common now. Seen mostly over hills and mountains, they are responsible for 8 per cent of UFO cases.

The triangle – this is a triangular-shaped object that appears as a silvery dark mass that moves slowly by day, and it appears as three lights in a triangular formation when seen by night. They have been observed across Africa and Europe and they have also been spotted in New York and England, particularly around Cheshire, Wales, Staffordshire and Leicestershire. Quite rare, it accounts for just 8 per cent of cases.

UFOs are not just spotted on land; they have also been seen around large bodies of water, especially in areas such as the Bermuda Triangle and off the east coast of Japan. This could possibly be as a result of the unique magnetism of these areas that may attract them. The most common type of UFO seen in these areas is the 'Saturn shape', a type that is also commonly encountered during abduction cases.

Chart Depicting Percentages of UFO Types – Results of Robert Bigelow's Survey:

TOP UFO HOTSPOTS	LOCATION
Africa	The Canary Islands
North America	The Niagara region
	The North-west Frontier
	Texas Triangle
South America	The São José, São Paulo
	Brazil mountains
	Argentina
	Puerto Rico
Asia	Japan's far North
	Malaysian Peninsula
Europe	Belgium
	Spain
	North-East Italy
	France
UK	Luce Bay – Scotland
	Lothian – Scotland
	South-west Dyfed – Wales
	Warminster
	Wiltshire
	The Pennines
	Hampshire
	Cornwall

Aliens and Area 51:

Possibly one of the most famous UFO stories is that of the mysterious aircraft that crashed near Roswell in New Mexico in 1947. Civilians arrived at the scene, only to find dead and injured alien bodies. When the military arrived, they captured the craft and the aliens and what followed was one of the greatest cover-ups in history.

It wasn't until US congressman Steve Schiff demanded the release of official documents and film footage relating to the incident that the events of 'Roswell' really came to light. The film footage showed the autopsy of two of the alien corpses and public interest soon stepped up. Some maintain that it is nothing more than an elaborate hoax, yet many believe it is one of the most important scientific discoveries in history. The Roswell footage shows bodies, which some sceptics claim look too human. Biologists, however, state that this is not unusual.

For example, chimpanzees share 98.4 per cent of human genes and yet they look 'less' human than the aliens in the film footage, suggesting that their DNA must be remarkably similar to that of human beings.

According to research studies, thousands of individuals have reported being abducted by aliens and they have often described being subjected to medical examinations. Ufologists believe that it could in fact be possible for aliens to take DNA samples from human beings during these experiments, thus creating more humanised versions of their own species. This may seem like a 'far-fetched' theory, yet it is one that attempts to explain the phenomenon that so many people claim to have experienced. Those that believe the aliens were real include witnesses of the event.

Several local Native American children witnessed something unusual on 31 May 1947, claiming to have seen a 'bright' light in the sky just moments before the crash. It was so strong that the children suffered blisters and burns on their arms, having shielded their eyes from the strong glare. Their description is said to fit with that of the 'cameraman's' and is linked with the events that later unfolded.

Another eyewitness account came from a rancher named William Brazel, who heard a loud explosion whilst in the vicinity of where the aircraft had crashed. The next day, he had discovered some wreckage scattered in the desert. He explained that what he had found was 'very light' and 'shiny in appearance' and that he had also, whilst examining it, found strange symbols on the tough, yet pliable material. Brazel went on to notify the local airbase at Roswell and Intelligence Officer Jesse Marcel collected the debris and it was flown to Wright-Patterson Air Force Base in Dayton, Ohio, for a more thorough investigation. There are claims that the Roswell material still exists in Ohio, along with the alien bodies that were found, and they are said to be kept in a secure facility – although its location is unknown.

Many ufologists believe that the 'alien landing' was real and they also claim that the US Government knows more about the aliens than we are led to believe. Some researchers suggest that in Area 51, there are secret underground bunkers in which aliens reside, and that in the Groom Lake facility, spacecraft are regularly tested and various experiments carried out.

Sceptics suggest that the 'Roswell air crash' was just a hoax, possibly carried out by the government and the military. They say that the spacecraft was actually created in a secret location in Groom Lake and that the aliens were simply latex dummies, whilst scientists suggest a more sinister explanation in that the aliens were actually 'doctored' human bodies, with certain known medical conditions. It is clear that for the Area 51 case, opinion is very much divided. What remains unclear though, is whether or not the events that occurred in 1947 depicted a true alien encounter.

Alien Abductions:

There are many people who claim to have been the victim of an alien abduction and there is widespread belief that aliens travel to Earth to carry out experiments on a chosen few.

Robert Bigelow, supporter of paranormal research, part-financed a survey on alien abductions which was carried out on over 5,947 respondents in the United States, who had reported undergoing various experiences as outlined below.

Not all participants claimed to have been abducted by aliens, for some experienced the sensations during out-of-body experiences, but those who had reported alien abduction all described similar events:

• Waking up paralysed with a sense of a strange person or presence being with you.
• Experiencing a feeling of being lost for an hour or more and not being able to remember why, or where, you have been.
• Feeling that you were flying through the air.
• Seeing unusual balls of light in a room, without knowing the cause of them.
• Finding scars or marks on your body that were not there before and neither you nor anyone else knows where they came from.

Acknowledging four of the five aforementioned 'symptoms' was taken as being evidence of alien abduction. Often, victims could only remember parts of their experience and they reported a feeling of disorientation following the event and some of these abductees have undergone hypnosis in the hope that more information could be revealed. Critics retort that the questions were too 'oblique' to be indicative of anything, but no similar surveys have been undertaken in the United Kingdom.

However, if the figures were comparable, then it would mean that around one million Brits have been kidnapped by aliens.

More extreme cases of alien abduction consist of the victim finding marks and scars on their body that were not there before. The most dramatic types of physical evidence are the 'implants' that some abductees claim that the aliens have inserted into their arms or other parts of their bodies. Many of these implants have been examined and have been found to be magnetic.

Reports of alien abduction and experimentation have come from all over the world; however, it was those that took place across the Canadian border, east of Toronto, that evoked the most public interest. Several objects were seen in the sky hovering above electricity power lines by many different witnesses and a few days after this event, a teenage girl also witnessed a UFO sighting and felt compelled to walk into a field in the region. The girl could not remember what had happened and reported waking after a few minutes, only to discover that the UFO had disappeared. Investigation by the Canadian UFO Research Network found an area of flattened grass at the site, as if something had landed there, and radiation levels were found to be higher than normal. The teenager was put under regression hypnosis and she relived the alien abduction experience, which she described as being led into the landed spacecraft and medically examined. She alleged that blood had been extracted from her finger, which had an unexplained pinprick hole.

An astonishing account of 'implant' abduction took place in the United States in the year 2000. After setting off home from work, Mr Wladyslaw, whilst approaching his car, suddenly became aware of a large, metal object 'hovering' above him.

He describes it as being 'oval and long, with pulsating blue lights surrounding its sides'. Suddenly, a blue light engulfed Mr Wladyslaw and he became aware of being in a small room, with two 'beings' standing on either side of him. The beings, dressed in blue metallic jackets, escorted him down a corridor, where he arrived at another room.

Inside the room were many instruments and machines and the technicians in the room were dressed in tunics. Wladyslaw describes sitting in a soft armchair, not unlike a dentist's chair, and the 'beings' then proceeded to examine him, ordering him to turn his hands over with the palms facing up, and then down. Sometime after this, Wladyslaw awoke to find himself back home, unsure of how he had arrived there and with no idea as to how much time had passed.

It appears that there is physical evidence of an implant in his thumb, where a small protrusion of a hard substance appeared just below the surface after the abduction. Wladyslaw agreed to undergo an X-ray, whereby a small, metal object, about the size of a mustard seed, was discovered. Wladyslaw refused to have it removed, fearing he would be abducted again. He did, however, agree to undergo regressive hypnosis in an attempt to recover lost memories.

1. Borley church and churchyard, which alongside the now-demolished Rectory was a much haunted site. Apparitions are still seen in the grounds to this stay.

2. Loch Ness, Scotland: Site of the infamous 'Loch Ness Monster'.

3. Ghost ships such as this one are said to appear on the most haunted coastline in Great Britain – Goodwin sands, Kent.

4. TV ghost: The disturbing image of a demonic face seen on this television screen is said to have appeared after it had been switched off.

5. Orbs/Fairy lights are the most frequently photographed par normal phenomena. Several orbs can be seen here in this Irish Woodland.

6. Crop Circle: One of the largest crop circle formations in Wiltshire.

7. A headless phantom dog is said to have haunted the streets of Central Manchester during the early 19th century. It was seen many times in and around the grounds of Manchester Cathedral. An Apparition of a woman has also been seen in the Cathedral.

8. Manchester Cathedral and the alley where the spectre of headless hound 'Shuck' was seen in 1825 by a Tradesman. It reputedly followed people, jumping up at them-until the creature was finally exorcised under the bridge over the river Irwell.

9. Shakespeare Hotel public house, Manchester: The ghosts of two young maids are said to haunt this city centre pub.

10. The Blue Bell Inn, Chester: The oldest domestic building in the city of Chester is said to be haunted by the ghost of 'Henrietta' who tragically took her own life in the cellar in 1645.

11. Coach and Horses public house, Chester: Home to a rather mischievous poltergeist and an 'old regular' who enjoys visiting the pub he frequented in life.

12. UFO: Spotted in the Sao José mountains, Brazil.

13

Crop Circles

Perhaps the earliest incident in which crop circles were put on record is the 'mowing devil' report from 1678 in Hertfordshire.

The circle was said to have mysteriously appeared after a farmer had had an argument with someone over the price he had quoted for the mower. In a fit of rage, the farmer had declared that he would rather the devil himself mow his oats.

Later that night, passers-by saw a fiery light in the field and a circle was found the next morning.

Since then, there have been more frequent sightings of crop circles. Indeed, they became more popular in the 1980s, when the number of sightings multiplied and the markings within them became much more complex; however, many of these circles were noticeable fakes. It seems that since the 1990s, the mystery surrounding UFOs had entered a new phase and an increasing number of 'mysterious swirled circles' began to appear in crop fields around the world, some becoming evermore intricate.

A spate of crop circles began to turn up in the UK at about this time and more than 1,000 circles were reported. Simple crop circles known as crop rings also started to appear, where the ring is flattened into a circular band, with the centre remaining unaffected. This type of crop circle is much less common; however, an example was found in Somerset by researcher Robert Moore in August 1991.

Although many crop circles are obvious fakes – the most famous hoax being the 'smiley face' that appeared in Wiltshire during the summer of 1990 – research shows that many are too complex to create without the use of specialist machinery.

Many scientists, however, believe that crop circles are not a supernatural phenomenon, but the result of an entirely natural, atmospheric occurrence. Professor Stephen Hawking claims that vortices form in the air when it is humid and calm, usually early in the morning or late at night.

Supporting this idea are professors John Snow and G. Terence Meaden, who have studied eddies of wind. They state that when the vortices move towards the ground, they sweep out circles in the crop fields. This could explain why crop circles are mostly found during hot summer months, when the air is humid, and it may also be the reason why they seem to occur during the night or in the early part of the morning. It doesn't, however, explain the intricate designs of most crop circles, as it is impossible for a vortex to create such patterns, and as a result, many ufologists and paranormal enthusiasts are not satisfied with the scientific explanation.

Paranormal investigators point out that in some cases, bends in the corn within the circle occur at the node, while 'hoax' formations produce a crack in the stem. The corn is also flattened in groomed layers, rather than appearing crushed, like in the hoax circles. Many reports state that crop formations are often accompanied by sightings of unusual lights or aircraft over the field late at night, where the following day, in the early part of the morning after the sightings had taken place, crop circles had appeared. Electromagnetic dysfunction was also reported in many cases, with witnesses claiming that their television sets and other electronic devices had malfunctioned during the night in incidents where crop circles had been formed nearby.

The night before the appearance of the 1991 Barbury Castle triangular crop formation, residents in the nearby village of Broughton experienced a power blackout. Compasses, EMF meters and dowsing rods all suggested that there were strong magnetic fields surrounding the crop circles and residual radiation was also detected, which can have adverse effects.

Measurements detected an emission of energy at the 5 kHz frequency for up to several days after the crop circles were formed. This frequency lies within the audible range and some witnesses claim to have heard a 'trill vibration' sound.

Many people show physical reactions after visiting crop circles and these symptoms include nausea, headaches, dizziness, tingling sensations and various pains. These symptoms are typical of the health problems associated with radiation exposure. On many occasions, mobile phones, cameras, watches and electronic equipment brought in to check the circles have all failed.

In the year 2000, crop circle researcher Colin Andrews made a controversial statement claiming that 80 per cent of crop circles were likely hoaxes. However, mystery surrounds the 20 per cent of 'unexplained' formations. It is interesting to note that the percentage filed as being 'genuine crop circles' tend to be positioned near the Earth's magnetic energy lines, either where ley lines intersect or on ancient sacred sites. Paranormal enthusiasts believe this is no accident.

The mystic origins of crop circles lie within the Avebury area of southern England, where many crop circles have been discovered around ancient sites such as earth mounds, the white horse hills and stone circles.

14

Ley Lines

A ley line is a straight fault line in the earth's tectonic plates.

The ley lines and their connecting intersection points resonate electromagnetic energy and it is believed to be this reason as to why so much paranormal activity occurs on ley-line sites. Ley lines align ancient monuments and megaliths (structures made up of large stones), churches and cathedrals, castles and battlegrounds; indeed all sorts of places that were once seats of power, religious worship or battle sites. Because of this, reports of ghost and UFO sightings around areas with ley lines are popular. In some cases, there is simply a negative or weird feeling surrounding the place. UFOs are said to travel along ley lines and it has been found that UFO sightings and abductions generally occur on sites where ley lines are prevalent. Research shows that 95 per cent of paranormal sightings/activity has taken place on sites where ley lines exist.

In 1921, amateur archaeologist Alfred Watkins brought the subject of ley lines into the public eye and later on, his ideas were adapted by other writers. Peter Underwood investigated several sites, focusing especially on areas where underground streams were prevalent. Underwood claimed that the crossing of such negative water lines explained why certain sites were chosen as being sacred or holy, hence the discovery of so many of these double lines and crossings found on sacred sites. It appears that buildings constructed on 'crossed' ley lines often experience paranormal activity and negative energy as the Earth's magnetic energy becomes trapped. It is said that it is this same energy that attracts spirit and poltergeist phenomena.

During the investigation of the Enfield Poltergeist, thirteen ley lines that intersected the house were found by investigator Maurice Grosse.

Some researchers believe that the mass of electromagnetic energy causes 'ghostlike' apparitions to appear or objects to move, rather than simply attracting spirits to the site, thus creating a cause and an effect. Our ancestors have known about the existence of these lines for thousands of years. Indeed, the native Indians of America called the lines 'spirit lines' and they were used by their shaman who would meditate upon these lines in order to contact spirits.

In Britain, the Druids called them mystical lines and there is a belief that as ley lines can give off positive or negative energy, occultists and practitioners of black magic deliberately blackened the lines, resulting in an increase of negative energy.

Paranormal author Andy Collins wrote about this in his book entitled *The Black Alchemist*, claiming that groups carried out these rituals up and down the country. Despite strong evidence, sceptics classify ley lines as pseudoscience and they argue that ley lines were unplanned by ancient cultures and they therefore dismiss their association with paranormal activity. They claim that owing to the sheer amount of historic and prehistoric sites, finding straight, connecting lines is merely coincidence.

15

Spontaneous Human Combustion

The frightening phenomenon in which a living person inexplicably bursts into flames without any sign of external ignition has been the subject of scientific debate for at least 300 years. There have been hundreds of cases, whereby mysteriously burned bodies have been found, some reduced to a heap of ashes. Spontaneous human combustion or SHC is much more common than people think. Pathologist Dr David Price stated that he had 'encountered a case roughly every four years'.

A strange feature of SHC deaths is the phenomenal speed in which the flames engulf the body. Even more unusual is that flammable furniture and even clothing remains untouched by fire, even though the body, which is made up of 75 per cent water, is completely destroyed. The intensity of heat needed to burn a human body is around 2,000°F (the temperature of a crematorium fire). Even during cremation, recognisable bones still remain, which must be ground by hand, whereas during SHC, victims are reduced almost entirely to ashes. This makes the destruction of the body during SHC seem even more mysterious, especially when viewed in conjunction with what remains after SHC:

– The body is more severely burned than one that has been caught in a normal fire.
– In some cases, the torso is completely destroyed, whilst the bones are reduced to ashes.
– The burns are not distributed evenly on the body and outside objects, such as curtains, and in some cases clothing, remain untouched by fire.

–   Often, small portions of the body, such as a leg, remain unburned.

–   A greasy soot deposit is found on nearby walls close to the body.

There have been many reported cases of SHC and listed next are some of the most popular:

> The most famous SHC case occurred in St Petersburg, Florida, in which Mary Hardy Reeser, a 67-year-old widow, spontaneously combusted while sitting in her easy chair on 1 July 1951. The next morning, she was found by her neighbour in a blackened circle, about 4 feet in diameter. The chair was intact and yet her body was reduced to ashes. All that remained was a skull and an undamaged left foot. This event captured much public interest in SHC and it also inspired many books on the subject.
>
> On 5 December 1966 in Pennsylvania, the ashes of Dr J Irving Bentley, aged ninety-two, were found in his bathroom. His body had inexplicably ignited and it had burned a 2-and-a-half by 3-foot hole through the flooring, leaving only a portion of one leg surviving, with his slipper remaining intact. Nearby paint remained unscorched.
>
> It has been noted that one of the earliest documented SHC cases occurred on 9 April 1744, in which Grace Pett, aged sixty, an alcoholic residing in Ipswich, England, was found on the floor by her daughter, who claimed her body was like 'a log of wood consumed by a fire, without an apparent flame'. Nearby clothing was undamaged.

SHC is a very real phenomenon; however, it has also been used in many works of fiction as the literary record shows.

There are nine famous references to SHC in pre-1900 fiction:

–   *Wieland* – Charles Brockden Brown (1798)
–   *Knickerbocker's History* of New York – Washington Irving (1809)

- *Jacob Faithful* – Frederick Marryat (1834)
- *Le Cousin Pons* – Honore de Balzac (1847)
- *Redburn* – Herman Melville (1849)
- *Bleak House* – Charles Dickens (1853)
- *Confessions of an Opium Eater* – Thomas de Quincey (1856)
- *Life on the Mississippi* – Mark Twain (1883)
- *Le Docteur Pascal* – Emile Zola (1893)

There are many different plausible theories as to the cause of SHC:

Alcoholism – many SHC victims have been alcoholics; however, this theory cannot be supported, as tests in the nineteenth century showed that flesh impregnated with alcohol would not burn with intense heat.

Body fat – some researchers claim that victims have been overweight; however, there have been just as many cases involving 'skinny' victims.

Build-up of static electricity – some scientists suggest that people with an above-average build-up of electricity in their bodies could feasibly combust, yet other scientists are adamant that no known form of electrostatic discharge could cause a human to burst into flames.

Poor diet – an explosive combination of chemicals can form in the digestive system from the consumption of food, such as eggs, which are rich in phospholipids, thereby adding to the methane and hydrogen already found in the gut.

Electrical fields – electromagnetic energy, which exists within the human body, may be capable of 'short circuiting', causing an atomic reaction which, in turn, could generate internal heat. This theory is supported owing to the significant number of cases which coincided with local peaks in the Earth's magnetism. High geomagnetism contributes to radio waves and this could suggest why SHC victims burn from the inside outwards.

Divine intervention – centuries ago, people believed that this phenomenon was a sign from God, given as divine punishment, and that it even featured in the Bible – 'By the blast of God they perish, and by the breath of his nostrils are they consumed,' (Job, 4:9).

Despite many scientific theories and ongoing investigations of SHC, no satisfactory explanation has ever been given and so therefore, this frightening phenomenon remains very much an unsolved mystery.

16

Black Magic, Witchcraft And Voodoo

The origins of Witchcraft:

Witchcraft and magic have been practised around the world for centuries. From the second millennium BC, the practice of black and white magic had been well established. Even the Bible makes mention of witches, condemning them. This led to the justification of burning, drowning and torturing so-called witches. It is fact that seven out of every ten people accused of being witches were women, many of whom were spinsters or 'old hags', who perhaps looked or behaved oddly but were, in fact, innocent.

In the sixteenth and seventeenth centuries, around 100,000 people in Europe were accused of being witches and were killed. 'Ducking' was a popular method used to assess a person for witchcraft, in which the suspected witch would be ducked into a nearby river or stream and if they floated, they were guilty and taken out to be executed. If, however, they sank, they were deemed innocent, but died from the drowning.

The infamous witch-hunts of Salem are well known, yet compared with the great witch-hunts of Europe, those of Salem were not widespread. In the English county of Essex, Witch-finder General Matthew Hopkins sent twice as many victims to the gallows as those in Salem. Salem, however, stands out owing to the sheer rate in which the fear of witchcraft spread throughout the village. It is said to have begun in 1691, when seven young girls situated in Salem village, Massachusetts, USA, decided to experiment with fortune-telling. They created a 'crystal ball' by pouring an egg into a wine glass and then they used this to see if they could conjure up images of their future husbands. What at first seemed like an innocent bit of fun was to turn into something quite grim.

When the daughter of Rev. Parris, Betty, began experiencing violent fits shortly after the experiment, her father put her through vigorous fasting and prayer. The other girls were also affected, suffering from hallucinations, choking attacks and loss of appetite. We now know that these are all classic symptoms of hysteria; however, in those days, the local doctor announced that the girls had become 'bewitched'. Some ten months later, twenty people (fourteen women and six men) were executed for witchcraft, while over 100 more were thrown into prison. One man refused to plead guilty to the charges and was pressed to death with rocks. By the time the witch-hunt of Salem had run its course, families' lives had been ruined, their homes destroyed and the name of the village tainted, becoming synonymous with mindless persecution.

Salem wasn't the only place where such hysteria against witches occurred. Indeed, throughout England, there have been numerous recorded witch trials:

Exeter – Temperance Lloyd, Mary Trembles and Susanna Edwards all confessed to witchcraft and were sentenced to death by hanging in 1682 in the town of Bideford.

Fressinfield – hysteria spread after the unexpected death of a baby. Here, many were accused of witchcraft, tried and executed.

Faversham – the trial of Joan Williford took place here in 1645 after she confessed to practising witchcraft. She also named others, who were executed along with her.

Somerset – was the site of two supposed witch covens during 1664.

St Osyth – was where fourteen people were charged for witchcraft practices.

Lancaster – two large trials were held here; one in 1612 and the other in 1633, in which thirty people lost their lives, many of whom were innocent.

The Pendle witches of Lancashire were the most famous witches in English history. The Lancaster witch trial of 1612 saw ten men and women hanged for witchcraft. The Pendle witches, as they became known, were believed to have been responsible for the murder of seventeen people in and around the forest of Pendle. There were thirteen witches in total: Alizon Device, Elizabeth Device, James Device,

Elizabeth Demdike, alias Anne Chattox, Anne Redferne, Katherine Hewitt, Alice Nutter, Jane Bulcock, John Bulcock, Isobel Robey, Jennet Preston and finally, Margaret Pearson.

The method in which they murdered their victims was described by Elizabeth Demdike during her confession, where she stated that they made an effigy of their intended victim, which was then burned over a period of time, causing the victim to fall ill and die. Demdike, who was in her eighties, was head of the Device family and was rumoured to be a very powerful witch. She had once been the close friend of Anne Chattox; however, they fell out and feuded bitterly. After Demdike had died, Chattox changed her story, claiming that Demdike was responsible for leading her into witchcraft.

Chattox was, however, accused of digging up three skulls from a nearby churchyard to use in a spell and was later hanged.

The majority of the evidence came from the confessions of four of the accused: Alison Device, James Device (her brother), their grandmother Elizabeth Demdike and her enemy Anne Chattox. It is interesting to note that Alison Device gave her account of witchcraft voluntarily, believing herself and her family to be guilty. The remainder of the Pendle witches, however, incriminated each other in the hope of saving themselves.

So much is known about the Pendle witches as a result of the proceedings of the Lancashire trial, which were recorded by the clerk of the court Thomas Potts and were later published in his book *Discovery of Witchcraft* in the County of Lancaster.

Witch Ghosts:

Not surprisingly, given the amount of lives lost during the witch-hunts, many places where they took place are said to be haunted. In Buxted, Sussex, there is a lane called Nan Tuck's lane. Nan Tuck was accused of being a witch and the villagers allegedly tried to drown her. Nan escaped, but was later found hanging from a tree in a nearby wood. Her ghost can still be seen running along the lane to reach the safety of the church to this day.

At Seafield Bay, Suffolk, it is said that the screams of witches tortured by the Witch-finder General can be heard in the dead of night. Three farmhouses on Pendle Hill, said to be where the Pendle witches held their Sabbat, are also reputedly haunted and they attract a large number of visitors every Halloween. Paranormal investigators have also frequented the farmhouses and surrounding area and Pendle Hill continues to be associated with witchcraft today.

Influential Occultists:

Between the years of 1480 and 1680 there was a deep interest in the type of ritual magic taught in the books of spells called grimoires. The exact origin of the very first grimoire is unknown; however, works similar to them existed in Ancient Egypt, with many also becoming widely available in the latter centuries of the Roman Empire. It is believed that the European grimoires were derived from these, as they show strong evidence of Jewish influences, with many attributed to King Solomon, master of magic. After 1800, this interest declined and such practices dwindled. There were, however, a handful of individuals who continued to experiment, sometimes to ill-effect. Many attempted to conjure up spirits and in the process, they invoked unwanted entities that they were unable to control.

Despite this, there was a small revival of ritual magic at the turn of the nineteenth century. In 1801, Francis Barrett, an occultist (1780 –1814), published a textbook entitled *The Magus of Celestial Intelligences.* This book included sections on natural philosophy, natural magic, the Kabbalah, astrology and physiognomy (the art of interpreting human character from facial appearance).

Throughout the nineteenth century, English occultists studied Barrett's work and experimented with ritual magic, in which more and more elaborate rituals involving the raising of spirits and the making of an 'astral shroud of darkness' (obtaining invisibility) were undertaken. One of the most prolific occult orders was the Order of The Golden Dawn founded in 1888 by occultists S. L. MacGregor Mathers, Dr William Wynn Wescott and Dr Robert Woodman.

The Golden Dawn did not focus purely on ritual magic, instead requiring the individual to gain knowledge through spiritual progression, thus leading to true wisdom and perfect happiness. However, its members were far from happy, as they wanted to study ritual magic and occult practices and so Mathers produced instructional material outlining the system of ritual magic that he, himself, had experimented with.

After the eventual collapse of the Golden Dawn, many turned their backs on ritual magic. However, today, even in the UK, there are groups and individuals still practising Golden Dawn magic. It certainly seems that witchcraft and magical practices were most prolific during the 1600s, for in the seventeenth century, Western witchcraft, alchemy and astrology began to be influenced by the Jewish mystical system known as the Kabbalah (Hebrew for tradition). The roots of Kabbalah can be found in the tenth century, when it was practised by over a million people in Ancient Israel. Much of it was concerned with power and the meaning of numbers in the Hebrew Scriptures and it is believed that the understanding of the Kabbalah ultimately brings man spiritually closer to God and as a result, man can be empowered with a higher insight, enabling prophecy and even control over nature.

At the heart of the Kabbalistic system is the Tree of Life – a geometrical arrangement of ten spheres called sephiroth, each associated with a divine attribute and twenty-two paths connecting the spheres. The Order of The Golden Dawn applied this to their teachings, as did many other occult orders.

Barrett's teachings were heavily influenced by the Kabbalah and he outlined the belief that the inner structure of the soul is reflected in the Kabbalah Tree of Life and the four types of Kabbalah knowledge: creation, functioning, ruling and reincarnation. Astrology also featured in his teachings and most astrologers cast and use a horoscope to depict planetary placements, which influence our daily activities. Kabbalistic astrologers take on a slightly different approach though, observing the planets as they relate to each of the ten sephira in the Tree of Life.

Studies of this mystical system continued to influence occultists throughout the 1800s. The French occultist Alphonse-Louis Constant, better known by his pseudonym as the magical writer Eliphas Lévi, studied it extensively. Born in 1810, Lévi grew up searching for a purpose in life. He devoted all his time to the church and later became involved in revolutionary politics. It was, however, upon meeting Polish mystic J. M. Hoene-Wronski, that Lévi found his true forte and strove to become the world's greatest ritual magician.

By 1810, J. M. Hoene-Wronski believed that he had reached the perfect understanding of ultimate reality and truth and as a teacher of mathematics, Wronski expressed his ideology through mathematical formulae. But he became unpopular owing to his sheer determination to attain grants and subsidies in order to support his work. At this point, it was unknown that Wronski was a student studying Gnosticism and the Kabbalah.

It was 1850 when Wronski first met Eliphas Lévi, who was so enamoured by Wronski's doctrine of the Kabbalah and other mystical systems that he decided to study the entire occult, such as alchemy, fortune-telling, magic and astrology. Lévi came to believe that ancient texts of alchemy and magic were written in secret code and upon deciphering this, he would learn the secrets of the universe.

A year after Wronski's death in 1853, Lévi decided to test his occult abilities by summoning the spirit of the first-century philosopher, explorer, and social reformer, Apollonius of Tyana. After three weeks of purification and preparation, Lévi evoked Apollonius three times, enabling him to ask the spirit profound questions about the universe. Unfortunately, the questions and answers were not recorded, so from a sceptical point of view, it is impossible to say whether or not the event actually took place. However, it is interesting to note that Lévi warned others about the dangers of carrying out similar occult experiments, claiming that he had experienced extreme exhaustion and shock at the time.

It was only after Lévi's experiment that he published *The Dogma and Ritual of High Magic.*

This book contained accurate accounts of alchemy, ceremonial magic, divination and astrology. However, details within the book were not accurate, which has led many to believe that Lévi deliberately distorted them in order to produce a more exciting read. His accounts, therefore, were deemed unreliable, leading many of his followers to seek out the works of other occultists, such as Madame H. P. Blavatsky and Aleister Crowley.

A part of Lévi's most influential ideologies was his belief in three fundamental theories – named by him as 'dogmas'. He claimed that these dogmas or theories explained all aspects of paranormal phenomena. The first of these theories is the 'Dogma of Correspondence'. This theory holds with the belief that the human soul is a microcosm or miniature universe, which reflects the nature of the macrocosm or great universe in which we live.

Therefore, by means of occult practices, the magician can change the outside world by changing the smaller inside one.

This link between worlds is the 'astral light', which forms the basis of the second dogma. Lévi believed that every physical object has an astral twin and upon manipulating the astral light, paranormal phenomena can occur. This can manifest itself in physical phenomena, such as the table-tipping/turning carried out by spiritualist mediums, and can therefore be achieved by the trained human imagination.

The third dogma explains how such imagination and willpower, when properly harnessed, can make the individual capable of producing spectacular 'magical effects'. During his lifetime, Lévi's theories attracted little attention, yet today, many regard him as one of the most influential occultists of all time.

Aleister Crowley is one of the most infamous Englishmen of the twentieth century. Deemed 'the wickedest man in the world', Crowley believed that he was the 'Beast' from the book of Revelation. Aleister Crowley, a dedicated occultist, practised ritual magic during the 1920s. He discredited spiritualist mediumship, yet had a total belief in magic.

Edward Alexander Crowley – later adapting his name to the unusual spelling of Aleister – was born in October 1875. Both of his parents were members of the Plymouth Brethren – a strict Protestant sect. Crowley was brought up to believe that every word in the Bible was the literal truth and that the Catholic and Anglican churches were 'synagogues of Satan'.

This strict religious upbringing undoubtedly had a profound effect on Crowley and following his father's death in 1887, his mother grew ever more vitriolic towards her son, deeming him as the 'Great Beast' from the book of Revelation.

Crowley did everything he could throughout his life to live up to this image and even came to believe that he was the Biblical beast. He grew up to resent Christianity and developed a deep hatred of the Brethren. In October 1895, at the age of twenty-one, he inherited a fortune of £30,000. He became a student at Trinity College, Cambridge, and during his three years at university, he became interested in the occult. Crowley studied the writings of Eliphas Lévi and gained inspiration from him, even coming to believe that he was the reincarnation of Lévi and that he would even surpass him in ritualistic magic.

In 1898, Crowley became a student member of The Hermetic Order of the Golden Dawn and came to admire two particular members of the society, Cecil Jones and Allan Bennett, the latter of whom shared a flat with Crowley in London. Together, they carried out a number of occult experiments. Many of these practices were carried out in the 'white temple'; a room lined with mirrors and devoted to white magic. However, his flat also had another room named 'the black temple', in which the altar was supported by the statue of a black man that was said to contain a skeleton. It was here that Crowley sacrificed sparrows and other small animals at the temple devoted to the dark arts of 'black magic'.

In 1900, the Golden Dawn split into two competing factions and Crowley was expelled. This ultimately led to Crowley losing interest in all aspects of Western occultism and instead, he moved towards Eastern traditions, in particular yoga and tantric practices which, in time, played a pivotal role in his creation of Sex Magick. Crowley embarked on travelling around the world, where he met Rose Kelly, who he called 'Ouarda the seer'. The couple married and in March 1904, whilst on their honeymoon in Cairo, Crowley, eager to prove his occult capabilities, carried out a number of magical rites.

He claimed to have received a psychic message from some unknown source telling him that a new epoch in history was about to begin and that he had been chosen as the prophet for this new age. His wife also received a message instructing that her husband was to sit down for one hour on three consecutive days with a pen and paper. The gods would then dictate the Gospel of the New Age to him.

Crowley followed these directions and heard a voice from a discarnate intelligence, 'Aiwass' (the god Seth), that dictated a prose that came to be known as *The Book of the Law*. The main message of this obscure text was that Crowley was to become the prophet of a new era – The Age of Horus. This new age was to replace the passing 'Age of Osiris', with its Christian faith. In the New Age, all religions such as Christianity, Islam, Hinduism and Buddhism would be replaced with a new faith of self-fulfilment. Crowley was told that 'Every man and woman is a star' – meaning that each individual has the right to develop in his or her own way – and 'Do what thou wilt shall be the whole of the Law' and 'The word of sin is restriction'.

Aleister Crowley believed that the true source of all wisdom was Seth, who was later worshipped as Satan. The brother of Osiris – the Ancient Egyptian god of the underworld – Seth killed and dismembered his body whilst in a jealous rage. He scattered the remains all over the land

and it was Isis, Osiris' wife, who pieced him back together again. This confrontation continues to fascinate occultists, as it is seen as the ultimate battle between the forces of good and evil. Crowley claimed that Seth had appeared to him while he was in Cairo, as well as dictating three chapters of *The Book of the Law* to him. Whilst in Egypt, Crowley looked for revelations in The Cairo Museum.

Upon discovering exhibit 666 – a painted tablet commemorating an Egyptian Priest Ankh-f-n-Khonsu – Crowley became convinced that he had been Ankh-f-n-Khonsu in a previous life.

Whilst in Egypt, Crowley also claimed to receive messages from Thoth, scribe of the gods, who figured in the ceremony of 'the weighing of the heart'; a ritual passage whereby Anubis (god of the dead) weighed the dead person's heart against a feather on the 'Scales of Justice'. Aleister Crowley later published a commentary on the Tarot he called *The Book of Thoth*. Between 1909 and 1914, Crowley caused a furore when he published secret documents of The Golden Dawn. The ten large volumes entitled *The Equinox* were a collection of stories, poems and occult material that led to Crowley ending up in court. Crowley, however, won the case in the Court of Appeal, as he was no longer a member of the order, although some believe magic played a part, as he consecrated a magical talisman in order to win favour with the judges.

In 1909, Crowley divorced his wife Rose, as she had become an alcoholic. Their daughter had died and eventually Rose Kelly ended up in an asylum, where she died as a result of her addiction.

It was after this that Crowley began to refer to all his mistresses as 'scarlet women'. By 1910, Crowley devoted his life to spreading the message of *The Book of the Law*. His published pieces that had featured in *The Equinox* spoke of Crowley's sexual excesses and it wasn't long before his homosexuality became common knowledge. He was fortunate enough to escape being thrown into prison, as homosexuality was still an offence at that time.

Soon after his wife's death, Crowley became involved with another magical order called The Ordo Templi Orientis (OTO), also known as The Knights Templar of The Orient. In 1910, Crowley was admitted into the first three degrees of this order. It was Crowley's involvement with this order that came to be the most significant in his career. Crowley became head of the English and Irish chapters and it was throughout his stay in America during the First World War that he incorporated the Law of Thelema, thus replacing the previous Masonic links with the OTO and rendering them obsolete.

In 1920, upon returning to Europe, Aleister Crowley established The Abbey of Thelema in Cefalu on the island of Sicily. For a time, Crowley enjoyed a modest success with a number of disciples visiting the abbey. The abbey became well established and Crowley had a succession of 'scarlet' women during this time. In 1922, Crowley published *Diary of a Drug Fiend*, a semi-autobiographical account of a man and his new wife, who toured Europe in a drug-fuelled haze. It was in 1923, however, that Crowley's successes were to come crashing down.

Oxford genius Raoul Loveday died at the abbey and his wife claimed that her husband had been poisoned by the cats' blood he had drunk during an occult ritual. Loveday's wife Betty May informed the authorities and later, the newspapers.

She spoke of drug-fuelled orgies, with children being exposed to sexual practices and bestiality. Crowley neither confirmed nor denied this; however, it was later to emerge that Loveday drank contaminated water and contracted enteritis.

Crowley had previously warned him of this fact, as sanitation on Cefalu was very poor; indeed, Crowley himself became ill on a number of occasions whilst on the island and his daughter Poupee, of one of his scarlet women Leah Hirsig, died.

Crowley quickly ran out of finances, as the number of people attending the abbey diminished. Following the death of Loveday, Crowley was expelled from Sicily. In 1929, he married again and continued to publish obscure books. He lived out the remaining years of his life struggling financially and was declared bankrupt in 1935. He did, however, continue his occult writings and created a set of Tarot cards, which were painted by Lady Frieda Harris. The work on the cards was expected to take three months but, instead, it took all of five years.

Aleister Crowley eventually died in Hastings in December 1947. He passed away hopelessly addicted to alcohol and heroin and as he died, he was said to have cursed his doctor, who mysteriously passed away soon afterwards. The legend of Aleister Crowley continues to this day and he has thousands of followers. It seems that his teachings are more relevant in present times than they ever were when he was alive.

Voodoo:

Voodoo, or vodun as its followers prefer it to be called, is a name attributed to a traditional West African spiritual system of faith and ritual practices. It is practised in south-eastern Ghana, Senegal and Burkina Faso and, more recently, it has spread to North and South America and the Caribbean. Voodoo's tradition of fables and faith stories are carried on through the generations and those who adhere to voodoo honour deities and ancient ancestors by way of ritualistic ceremonies.

Voodoo is the African word for 'spirit' and its origins can be traced back to the West African Yoruba people, who practised this faith during the eighteenth and nineteenth centuries.

However, this ancient religion has roots which go back as far as 6,000 years in Africa. Slaves brought the voodoo religion with them when they were shipped to Haiti and other West Indian islands and voodoo also helped to shape identity in the black Americas, which had previously been predominantly Roman Catholic. From Haiti, it spread to New Orleans and Mississippi and was renamed 'hoodoo'.

Voodoo was forced underground as a result of its suppression during colonial times, when many who practised voodoo were killed or imprisoned, as their 'religion' posed a threat to Christianity and Roman Catholicism. Voodoo and hoodoo are often mistaken for being one and the same thing; however, many believe that with the persecution of the voodoo religion, 'hoodoo' is what remains. True hoodoo is practised in Togo, Benin and Burkina Faso and in the US, hoodoo is not a religion but more a form of spiritual magic.

Today, over 60 million people practice voodoo and late at night on Rio de Janeiro's Copacabana Beach, many of the country's inhabitants can be found practising voodoo rites.

Although predominantly Roman Catholic, Brazil is also home to 65,000 voodoo temples, where spirit religions collectively known as macumba are practised. Macumbistas worship a host of exotic gods and demons, casting spells to bring wealth, love or power.

During such rituals candles are lit and worshippers dressed in white offer gifts to the goddess Yemanja – the daughter of heaven and earth; queen of the ocean. The candles are placed in a previously dug hole – which is carefully walled with sand to protect against wind – and, in turn, the worshippers can tell Yemanja their desires. If the favour is to be granted, the candles will be swept out to sea. If, however, they are blown out by the wind, the favour will not be granted. During this ceremony, worshippers begin the ritual by dancing; indeed, some of the dancers enter a trance-like state, becoming possessed. Often when returning to normal consciousness, the dancers cannot remember what happened during the trance.

Superstition plays an integral role in Brazilian culture. The belief in gods, demons and supernatural powers is particularly strong. Vodun priests – houngan or hungan (male) and mambo (female) – practise 'white' magic to bring good fortune and healing. However, there is a darker side to the spirit religion called Quimbanda, which is an evil form of voodoo in which worshippers called Caplatas practice black magic against their enemies. The main technique of Quimbanda is 'closing the paths', which involves casting a spell that prevents the victim from ever achieving happiness. The person afflicted by this spell becomes unlucky in love, finance and health and they can be seen to encounter seemingly never-ending problems.

A belief of vodun is that a dead person can be brought back to life after dying and controlled whilst in a 'zombie-like' state.

In reality, a zombie is a living person, who is under the influence of powerful drugs administered by an evil sorcerer.

Voodoo dolls are also synonymous with black-magic rituals and were once used as a method of cursing an individual. Such practices were widespread throughout New Orleans and still continue to this day in certain areas of South America.

The church condemns the practice of voodoo, because it is a polytheistic religion and as there is only one God, all other gods that are worshipped are therefore demons. It is also condemned owing to the use of occultism and the sacrilege of using saints to mask their 'demons', which confuses ignorant believers. Despite this, there are 20 million people who practise some form of voodoo in African countries and there are over 40 million Brazilians who combine Christian worship with macumba.

Perhaps it is these ceremonies that have helped Brazil to make a name for itself as 'land of paranormal phenomena'.

Indeed, the amount of UFO sightings and the sheer number of poltergeist phenomena that have taken place in this country and still continue to this day cannot be denied.

17

Vampires: Fact or Fiction?

Vampires were first made internationally famous by the Irish Author Bram Stoker with his 1897 novel Dracula. However, around the world there are many people who believe that vampires have existed throughout time and they also still believe that they are, in fact, still around today. The main focus of vampire lore comes from Eastern Europe; however, it has been discovered that in Roman cemeteries, bodies were buried with their heads pointing downwards, so they could not find their way out. It is also believed that graves from the Iron Age had large, heavy stones placed on top of buried corpses to stop them from rising after death.

In Chinese folklore, the undead are believed to rise up from their graves and stalk their victims if they have any unfinished business and Hindu literature talks of demons that appear only at night and drink the blood of infants. Sceptics believe that vampires simply represent the fears of people; however, archaeologists have recently claimed that they have proof that vampires really existed.

During excavations in the ancient town of Deultum, Bulgaria, archaeologists found sixteen skeletons with large nails driven through their bones. They believe that these were vampires were nailed to their coffins in order to stop them rising from the dead. Hundreds more bodies in a similar state to these were found in the mass graveyard of 'necropolis' and many believe this proves the existence of vampires. In 2001, archaeologists unearthed a tenth-century graveyard in the Czech Republic, where fourteen corpses had been buried in reinforced coffins, their skulls having been shattered by nails, stakes having been driven through their hearts and a knife having been plunged into their mouths. Could this simply be a result of fear that had been spread throughout Eastern Europe owing to the many legends and folklore stories about bloodsucking Draculas? It is certainly a fact that fear of vampires still thrives in this region today, where the majority of legends and sightings still arise.

Those who believe that vampires exist claim that the species arose in this area and that it was probably confined there until about 150 years ago. Recent evidence suggests that the larger cities within Eastern Europe attracted a fast-growing network of vampire communities and the most serious of researchers remain at work there, with just a few in the Carpathian Mountains, where vampires are also said to have been seen.

Vampire folklore within the British Isles is surprisingly scarce; however, there are a few documented cases said to have taken place mostly in earlier centuries:

> Alnwick Castle, Northumberland, in the eleventh/twelfth century – a vampire is said to have once frequented this castle, emerging at night to attack local villagers. An outbreak of the plague was also attributed to the creature, resulting in the villagers digging the monster up from its shallow grave and burning it.

> Croglin Low Hall, Cumbria, 1875 – this creature is said to have attacked a young girl within the building. One of her brothers witnessed the attack and shot the monster in the leg. They then followed the trail of blood, tracking it back to the village graveyard, where it was dug up and burnt.

> Thornton Heath, Surrey, 1938 – over a period of three months, a woman reported being attacked by a winged creature, which bit her neck and drew blood.

These events may sound frightening, but scientists state that the real roots of the vampire are based on a mixture of early beliefs and folklore concerning death and disease. In the past, little was known about diseases, especially those that struck without warning, so it was easy to blame them on a supernatural entity, which could then become the focus for everyone's anger and grief. It is interesting to note that the majority of 'vampire reportings' happened during the early centuries that were plagued with disease and where the belief in superstition ran high.

Scientists also point out that many of the bodies dug up from graves believed to have been vampires showed natural effects of decomposition. During the earlier centuries, nobody really knew this and believed that the red bloated appearance of the corpse meant that it had to be a vampire. Of course, nowadays, the effects of decomposition are well known: gases build up in the body causing it to become bloated, the blood breaks down, giving a deep red appearance, and the skin shrinks back making nails, teeth and hair appear longer.

Driving a stake through a body like this would lead to the rupture of gases and gore and during the resultant hysteria, the noise of escaping gas could easily have been mistaken for a groan.

However, despite this scientific analysis, the belief in vampires still exists today, with many Eastern Europeans claiming to have spotted them recently. Could this be the result of vampire stories being passed down through the generations, or could it be something more sinister? This is a question that, for the time being, remains unanswered.

18

Mysteries

There are still many unsolved mysteries from around the world that continue to interest not only paranormal investigators, but also cryptozoologists, who study unusual, profound creatures such as Bigfoot, the Loch Ness monster, the yeti and 'alien' big cats. This section explores such creatures rumoured to exist, but for which substantial proof is missing, and it also delves into other mysteries, such as ghost ships, Mothman and the disturbing accounts of animal mutilations. Included are opinions from scientists, sceptics and supporters of the paranormal, so that you, the reader, can consider all possibilities before making up your own mind:

- The Loch Ness Monster
- Bigfoot
- The Beast of Bodmin Moor
- Mothman
- Animal mutilations
- The Bermuda Triangle
- Ghost ships
- Mysterious showers from the sky
- Blood, water and tears

The Loch Ness Monster:

The mystery surrounding the infamous 'Loch Ness Monster' is by no means a recent one. The earliest written report of a 'monster' in Loch Ness was documented in AD 565, having been spotted by the Irish monk St Columba. At the time, he had been waiting for a boat to collect him, so that he could cross the loch; however, when it failed to turn up, it resulted in one of St Columba's disciples swimming across the mile-wide loch in order to reach a boat. Whilst doing this, he was amazed to see 'something like a huge frog suddenly rise to the surface of the loch with a great roar and an open mouth'.

There were several other witnesses, who are said to have been 'stricken with great terror', but St Columba merely made the sign of the cross and commanded the monster to disappear. After this, it is said that the monster 'sank beneath the loch's chilly waters'.

This is just one of the many reported sightings of the Loch Ness monster, although it seems that documented reports have declined over the years, especially since the 1960s and 70s, when the number of sightings and photographs were less than those in previous years. This in itself seems to be unusual, as more visitors nowadays are equipped with digital cameras. The whole story, however, really began when the number of sightings increased dramatically, peaking during the 1970s. It appeared that the strongest evidence by a long way was the eyewitness reports, resulting in news coverage on a large scale.

There were altogether 10,000 reported sightings, 3,000 of which had been recorded, of which 251 were regarded as being 'valid'.

On 22 July 1933, one of the most famous early sightings was reported by Mr and Mrs Spicer, who had claimed to have spotted the 'monster' on land, which was unusual in itself and was the only sighting of its kind. This case is mentioned in many books and on several websites. Scientific researchers state that as with all evidence, it is vital to read all published accounts, as well as full reports, before settling on any one opinion. Many simply discredit all reports and have several theories on what the monster may actually be. Some state that the '1933' case was probably a large grey seal. Other animals have also been suggested, such as dolphins, whales and, stranger still, a swimming elephant. None of these explanations have ever been proven and the mystery of the Loch Ness monster remains.

Bigfoot:

Bigfoot, also known as Sasquatch, is an unknown animal species said to inhabit areas within North America. He is described as a large, bipedal, hairy, hominid creature, said to be related to the yeti of Tibet and Nepal. The first reported sightings of Bigfoot were in 1924, but there were legends prior to this around the 1860s. In 1958, footprints were found in Humboldt County, California, that were too large to belong to any native creature. Similar footprints have also been discovered in Texas.

Perhaps the most famous Bigfoot footage is that which was taken in the Californian wilderness of Bluff Creek in 1967.

Roger Patterson and Robert Gimlin claimed that their film footage was genuine and while some regard it as the most important piece of evidence to date, others simply dismiss it as a hoax.

Bigfoot sightings have mostly taken place across North and South America, although some eyewitness accounts claim that they sometimes take place in conjunction with UFO sightings.

Bigfoot is one of the most famous creatures in cryptozoology, although this type of study of unusual creatures is dismissed by mainstream researchers. Very few scientists believe in the existence of hominids such as Bigfoot, owing to unreliable eyewitness accounts and a lack of physical evidence.

Most dismiss it as folklore and claim that the reports are hoaxes.

Although a great deal of evidence supports the existence of Bigfoot, its validity has always been questioned. Some theories have been put forward in an attempt to explain what Bigfoot might be, although such theories have received little support from many of the mainstream scientists. Fossils of a creature bearing a resemblance to Bigfoot have been found in China and this creature is said to be of the Gigantopithecus species and cryptozoologists claim that it is likely that such creatures may have migrated across to America and the Himalayas.

However, as the Gigantopithecus was a quadruped, it is unlikely to be an ancestor of a biped, as Bigfoot is said to be.

Sceptics discredit the existence of Bigfoot and similar creatures such as the yeti, as they stress how primates live in the tropics, Africa or continental Asia. Great Ape fossils have never been found in the Americas, where the majority of Bigfoot sightings take place; therefore, they claim that any evidence remains inconclusive. The great number of hoaxes substantially contributes to their beliefs and it is on this basis that many scientists refuse to give the subject any serious attention. There are, however, a few prominent scientists who have expressed an interest in Sasquatch reports, including Russell Mittermeier – vice president of Conservation International and chairman of the worldwide Primate Specialist Group – Daris Swindler – professor emeritus of anthropology at the University of Washington – and George Schaller – director of science for the Wildlife Conservation Society. Cryptozoologists and some anthropologists argue that creatures like Bigfoot deserve further study. It is interesting to note though, that the sightings continue. Recently, on 10 February 2007, an ape-like foot was found in a landfill site in Virginia. It was cleaned, X-rayed and examined at the state forensic lab and it has since become something of a modern phenomenon, leaving Bigfoot believers wondering if this may finally be proof of the creature's existence.

The Beast of Bodmin Moor:

It has been said that one of the most popular subcategories in cryptozoology is that of alien big cats, or ABCs as they are most commonly known. In this sense, 'alien' refers to large felines that are often spotted in places where they should not be. ABC sightings in Britain totalled 300 in 1996 alone and like other creatures such as Bigfoot, they invoke interest from many investigators and cryptozoological researchers.

The majority of sightings of these big cats appear to be around Cornwall, in South-west England, and Bodmin Moor became the epicentre of these sightings. Indeed, the quantity and frequency of reports by people claiming to have spotted the 'leopard-like' creature resulted in the naming of the big cat as The Beast of Bodmin Moor. Things began to get serious though, when several small animals and livestock in and around the area were found slain. As a result, The Ministry of Agriculture, Fisheries and Food launched an investigation in 1995. The results were interesting, as they stated that there was insufficient evidence to verify that such exotic felines do in fact exist in Great Britain and that the farm animals could easily have been attacked by any common species. However, the report concluded that the investigation could not prove that the big cat is not present.

Less than a week after the report, on 24 July, a young boy uncovered startling evidence that was to hit the national press.

Barney Lanyon-Jones, a 14-year-old boy from Bodmin Moor, was out walking with his brothers by the River Fowey at the southern-most edge of the moor, when Barney noticed what he thought to be an 'odd-shaped rock' bobbing about on the water, but when he pulled it out, he realised that it was in fact a large, feline skull. The skull measured 4 inches wide by 7 inches long and it appeared to have a missing lower jaw; however, one particularly identifiable feature was the two sharp, prominent incisors, which indicated that the skull could have been that of a leopard.

It wasn't long before the skull was handed over to London's British Museum of Natural History for examination, where it was confirmed as belonging to a young, male leopard. It was also uncovered that the animal did not, in fact, die in Britain, but could have been transported from overseas as a leopard-skin rug. The missing part of the skull suggested this, as it appeared to have been cleanly cut away, a process typically carried out when mounting the head on a rug. There was also an egg case that was found inside the skull that appeared to have been laid by a tropical cockroach.

These findings were a blow to all who believed that evidence had finally been found proving the big cats' existence and it was not the first time, either. In 1988, two teenage boys found a skull on Dartmoor that had also once been part of a rug and in 1993, a cat skull found in Exmoor was identified as being part of a taxidermy. Some experts in zoology suggest that these skulls could be deliberately planted as a hoax, as they are often found in areas where there have been reports of big-cat sightings. There is, however, other evidence to suggest the existence of ABCs, such as the large paw prints found in the soil on Bodmin Moor. When examined, it was concluded that they belonged to a puma and that the tracks were fairly fresh.

For many years, scientists refused to look into reports of ABC sightings, dismissing them as mistaken identification of other animal species or as being outright hoaxes.

In 1997, shortly after the discovery of the paw prints, something changed that made a breakthrough. An alleged photograph of the Bodmin Beast materialised, which showed an adult, female puma that appeared to be pregnant. Scientists and zoologists still concurred that this was not sufficient evidence; however, in August 1998, video footage taken on the moor showing the big cat provided a turnaround. The twenty-second-long video invoked interest from Newquay Zoo curator and wildcat expert Mike Thomas, who concluded that this was 'the best evidence yet'. He and a few other wildcat enthusiasts believe the animal could be a species of wildcat that is supposed to have become extinct in Britain more than a century ago.

Sightings of these 'alien' big cats still continue and since 1983, there have been over sixty sightings on Bodmin Moor alone, plus others in places further afield, such as Kent. There was a particular frenzy in 2004, when wildcats were spotted on over fifty occasions in southern Scotland. All reports show similarities, in that the creature is said to resemble a black panther or a puma, with its size ranging from 3 to 5 feet long for the body, with a tail measuring approximately 18 to 24 inches long.

In recent years, the possible existence of the Bodmin Beast has attracted interest from many paranormal groups. This is believed to be because the area is home to ancient stone circles, burial mounds and tracts of land shaped like figures of the zodiac. The area was also frequented by Knights Templar and was home to the legend of King Arthur. Some argue it is for that very reason that people report seeing these big cats, claiming that the mysterious surroundings stir people's imagination. This does not, however, explain sightings in other parts of Great Britain and neither does it account for the creatures shown on photographic and video footage. So the question remains: are there really 'alien' cats out there from bygone times? Why not visit Bodmin Moor and see if you can spot the infamous beast.

Mothman

Point Pleasant, West Virginia, is a hot spot for paranormal researchers eager to discover the mystery surrounding events that occurred there during the years of 1966 and 1967. Many of the people who live here believe that they have been witness to sightings of Mothman, UFOs and encounters of 'men in black'.

For almost a year, strange happenings continued in this area. Controversial author John Keel has written extensively about Mothman and he believes that it could in fact be the visitation of an 'elder god', in the same category as demons and angels. Whatever the creature is said to have been, it appears to have been no hoax. The only question was: who or what was responsible for the reign of terror inflicted upon the small town? There were hundreds of sightings of the Mothman and it all started on 15 November 1966, when two young couples were driving past an abandoned power plant. They reported seeing a large, black-winged humanoid, with glowing red eyes.

After this initial sighting, similar experiences were also reported. Indeed, small animals disappeared, television and other electrical equipment suffered from interference and many cars broke down on lonely roads. UFO sightings became popular over the Ohio River and witnesses reported seeing strange men in dark suits around the area.

Possibly one of the strangest and most frightening experiences of all was the collapse of the Silver Bridge that connected Point Pleasant, West Virginia, with the State of Ohio, on 15 December 1967, killing forty-six people. Many felt that the bridge disaster was a direct result of the strange phenomena that had blighted the small town for a year, as after the tragedy, all paranormal activity seemed to disappear. It was, however, later uncovered that a failure in the number 13 eyebar, a crucial part of the bridge's stability, was to blame. Some people argue that the Mothman was an 'omen' sent to warn people of the impending disaster, whilst others believe it was 'evil' that actually made the bridge collapse.

Many psychologists state that there could be a non-paranormal explanation. The government discovered in the 1990s that spills from old chemical factories flowed into the area, where ponds, streams and a bird sanctuary were situated.

Interestingly, this was also where the Mothman was sighted most frequently. It has been suggested that the creature may have been a sandhill crane that could have migrated south from Canada. These birds stand at over 3 feet tall and have red rings of feathers around their eyes. It could be a possibility that nuclear chemicals from the spill affected one of the birds and caused it to mutate, double in size and to act in an aggressive manner. There were certainly cases recorded of fish from nearby ponds being affected by the spill, so could this possibly be a rational explanation?

This explanation was put forward to witnesses, who rejected the idea, stating that what they saw looked nothing like a crane.

John Keel put forward a theory that some of the 'witnesses' could have been frightened by the reports and that what they actually saw was owls flying near deserted roads, later believing that they had seen the Mothman. However, it can be argued that there have been impressive, multiple witness sightings, which were deemed reliable by law-enforcement officials.

There are also questions surrounding the mysterious UFO sightings, strange lights, poltergeist activity, the 'men in black' and, most horrifying of all, the collapse of the Silver Bridge.

John Keel believes that Point Pleasant was a 'window area', a place marked by periods of strange sightings and UFO phenomena. He states that while the UFO and Mothman sightings were not directly responsible for the collapse of the bridge, there may well be a connection to the intense activity in the area at the time. Other paranormal researchers claim that the strange happenings were linked to the legendary 'cornstalk curse' that was said to have been placed on Point Pleasant in the 1700s.

It is believed that five men were in the local cemetery that day, preparing a grave for a burial, when something that resembled a 'brown human being' took off from some nearby trees and flew over their heads. The men were taken aback by this experience, as they were adamant that what they had seen did not appear to be a bird, but more like a 'man with wings'.

A few days later, more sightings took place in and around the same area. All witnesses described seeing the same thing: a man with wings that were too big to be a bird of any kind.

Nobody knows for sure the reasons why this strange being came to visit the quiet town of Point Pleasant or what, indeed, was responsible for the sudden poltergeist phenomena. Stranger still is the fact that all sightings stopped after the incident involving the Silver Bridge took place. Could this fatality have been directly linked with the 'cornstalk curse', or was it just an accident? Was the Mothman sent to warn the town of its impending disaster? These questions and many more are still put forward to paranormal investigators and the true identity of the Mothman is still very much a mystery.

Animal Mutilations:

Since the 1960s, animals have been found lying dead in fields, with their bodies appearing to be mutilated. Stranger and more macabre still is the fact that no blood or signs of a struggle have been found around the dead animal. Upon examining the bodies, it becomes clear that the marks found on the animal are not typical of predators, such as wolves.

Instead, the incisions made on the animal's body and the clean removal of the internal organs suggests surgical precision.

Cattle mutilation (also known as bovine excision) refers to the killing and the subsequent mutilation of cattle under anomalous circumstances. Sheep and horses have also been the victim of this type of mutilation.

The first animal mutilation to be reported took place on 9 September 1967 in the San Luis Valley of southern Colorado.

The Appaloosa, a breed of horse known for its spotted, patterned coat, was found dead and stripped of its flesh from the neck up. A pathologist confirmed that all of the chest organs had been cleanly removed by way of a heated instrument, such as a laser. Cattle are usually the main targets for 'animal mutilators', although many horses have also been the victims of these macabre murders. In 1993, a male calf was found dead in Harding County, South Dakota. A perfect circular incision had been made in the removal of the hide, navel, genitals and rectum. An ear, an eye, the bottom lip and the tongue had also been cut away. None of these parts were taken away, but they remained next to the animal and the precise cuts were clearly not made by any animal.

A microscopic analysis of the calf's blood showed that the haemoglobin had been 'cooked' by the intense heat from the cutting instrument. The organs were also found to be dry and bloodless. Investigators of these events suggest that there could be a variety of explanations for this, some of which are paranormal and others of which are rational. Scientists, veterinarians and agricultural workers suggest the following possible explanations:

- Missing parts of the mouth, genitalia and anus are explained as a result of dehydration; parasites then enter the body where the skin is at its thinnest.
- Missing eyes and organs are described as being the result of insects, such as blowflies or birds, such as the buzzard, that are known to gain entry to the internal organs through the eyes and the anus.
- The absence of blood is thought to be caused by the blood pooling in the lower parts of the body and breaking down into organic components. Insects could also feed upon the remaining blood outside of the body.

Paranormal investigators, however, disagree and suggest other explanations:

- The mutilations could be carried out by members of a cult.
- The mutilations are related to phases of the moon and certain days specific to pagan symbolism of fertility.
- The absence of blood may suggest that members of such a cult drink it.
- Unborn calves are removed from mutilated cattle.
- Organs are removed for use in rituals.

Some paranormal groups such as ufologists claim that the mutilations could be carried out by 'other worldly' beings, namely aliens, who carry out such acts as a means of collecting genetic material. These hypotheses are based on the premise that ordinary human beings could not perform such clean, precise incisions like those found on the mutilated animals in such a short space of time without being seen. The fact that no evidence has ever been left behind further reiterates this claim.

It is also interesting to note how the results of examinations and autopsies on the animals show the use of unconventional tools and other unexplained phenomena.

Reports collected by the FBI state that in many cases, UFOs and other unusual aircraft were often seen in the area just before or just after the mutilated animals were found. There is, however, no definitive answer as to why alien beings should carry out such mutilations on certain animals (mostly cattle), although some proponents have put forwards possible suggestions, such as the harvesting of body parts for use in experiments. This also links in with reports by alien abductees, who claim to have noticed incision marks and scars on their bodies directly following their experience.

A less conventional hypothesis has been put forward in an attempt to explain the mutilations, which concerns the large amount of mutilated cattle that were discovered in close proximity to former US nuclear-testing sites. It has been speculated that the military dissected cattle in order to determine the level of radioactive material in the animal's soft tissue, e.g. the mouth, the anus and the lower soft organs. By doing this, it would allow the military to gauge the level of radioactive exposure each animal had received, as well as giving them the opportunity to monitor the areas with the largest amount of radioactive fallout. As a result, it would allow the military and governmental agencies to estimate probable levels of human exposure to fallout and thereby roughly ascertain the amount of radioactive contamination entering the human food chain through milk and meat.

In the 1990s, a spate of animal mutilations in Puerto Rico and Mexico were said to be caused by the Chupacabra or the grotesque 'goatsucker' as it is commonly called. According to several eyewitness descriptions, the beast appeared to be '4 or 5 feet high, walking semi-bipedally, with spines running from its head to its back'. The sightings continue to this day, whilst the mutilations in Puerto Rico have largely died out. Many researchers agree that the animal attacks were most likely to be caused by a mongoose or similar creature, although some of the killings were said to be undoubtedly human cultist activity.

More recently, in April 2000, were the cases of animal mutilations in Calama, northern Chile. A spate of farm animal deaths, with over 300 mutilated animals, were reported, many of which had incisions in their throats. After much investigation, strange footprints were found near the site. Later on, more animal deaths occurred, with over thirty hens, ducks, pigs and dogs being found to be mutilated. The footprints were taken to an investigatory laboratory and although an exact match could not be found, they were described as being 'similar to dog prints'.

In the case of animal mutilation, this mysterious phenomenon is still an open book. There is only speculation and nobody has definite answers that can explain the cause of such grisly acts. Who do you believe? I will let you make up your own mind.

The Bermuda Triangle:

This is an imaginary area located off the south-eastern Atlantic coast of the United States. It stretches from the east coast of Florida to the island of Bermuda and back to Puerto Rico. It is famously noted for the high incidence of unexplained losses of ships, small boats and aircraft.

The first major account was that of Christopher Columbus.

As the Nina, the Pinta and the Santa Maria sailed through the area in 1492, it is reported that Columbus' compass went haywire and his crew witnessed the appearance of strange lights in the sky. It has been suggested, however, that the compass' inaccuracy was little more than the discrepancy between the north and magnetic north. The lights were said to have been a meteor; however, Columbus is said to have seen the lights again near the horizon on 11 October, the day before his famous landing.

Another historical event attributed to the Bermuda Triangle is the discovery of the Mary Celeste on 5 December 1872. The vessel was found abandoned, floating in the Atlantic Ocean about 400 miles off its intended course from New York to Genoa. There was no sign of its crew, its captain, Benjamin Spooner Briggs, his wife Sarah or their 2-year-old daughter Sophia, and since the lifeboat was also missing, it is possible that they abandoned ship during a storm. The cargo of industrial alcohol supplies remained on the boat, although with so many basic supplies having been left behind, there couldn't possibly have been enough on the lifeboat to last for any length of time.

To this day, nobody knows the real reason why the Mary Celeste was abandoned. However, Pieter van der Merwe of the National Maritime Museum believes that the likeliest explanation is that the crew abandoned ship during a storm and later perished on the lifeboat. Other suggestions have been put forward, such as those stating that the ship was cursed, as before Captain Briggs purchased the ship, it had been given a different name. He is said to have renamed and repainted it.

The mystery surrounding the Bermuda Triangle really made the headlines on 5 December 1945, with the famous vanishing of flight 19, in which five Navy Avenger bombers mysteriously disappeared while on a routine training mission. A rescue plane was sent to search for them, but this also vanished. A total of twenty-seven men and six aircraft had disappeared without a trace. Sceptics state that the airmen were 'inexperienced' and could simply have gone off course.

However, this does not explain where the men or aircraft disappeared to and why experienced patrol leader Lt. Charles Carroll Taylor failed to pass the mission.

Countless theories attempting to explain the many disappearances have been offered. Nautical explanations point to environmental factors and seamen and nautical experts discredit supernatural explanations. The majority of vanishings can be attributed to the unique magnetic fields in that area.

Indeed, the Bermuda Triangle is one of the two places on Earth where a magnetic compass points towards true north, the other being off the east coast of Japan, also famed for its disappearances. This is known as 'compass variation' and if this is not accounted for, navigators could find themselves far off course and in trouble.

Another environmental factor is the character of the Gulf Stream, which is extremely turbulent; indeed, the strong undercurrent could quickly erase all evidence of a disaster. The weather in this region is also unpredictable and thunderstorms, water spouts and eddies often spell disaster for pilots and mariners. The ocean floor here is also one of the deepest in the world.

The paranormal explanations are very different: curses, balls of fire and UFO sightings have all been linked to the Bermuda Triangle. A vast amount of speculation has surrounded such reports, the most controversial being that below this part of the ocean lies the lost city of Atlantis. UFO sightings in this area appear to be 'above average'; however, there have been other explanations for the constant appearance of strange lights and fireballs. Some suggestions have been put forward by scientists that they may be caused by an excess of methane gas, similar to that of the 'Marfa lights' phenomenon. The fireballs could in fact be ball lightning or St Elmo's fire – a corona discharge often seen above a ship's mast.

This would occur as a result of the magnetic fields in the Bermuda Triangle that are disturbed during frequent thunderstorms.

The theories put forward by nautical experts and scientists point towards forces of nature, which seems to outdo supernatural explanations, by offering logical theories and information explaining the phenomenon encountered in the Bermuda Triangle. However, although such explanations make sense, nobody really knows for sure the exact reasons for the many mysterious disappearances.

Ghost Ships:

There are said to be many ghost ships that haunt shorelines around the world, replaying their final voyages. There are two types of ghost ship: those that appear on the anniversary of their sinking and those that mysteriously appear at random, near shores, with no visible sign of any crew. Perhaps the most famous abandoned ship is the Mary Celeste, found entering the Bay of Gibraltar in 1872. Writer Sir Arthur Conan Doyle used some of the facts surrounding the mysterious ship and wrote a book, which helped to keep the story very much alive.

Ghost ships belong in the category of 'time slips'. Other types of phenomena that fall into this category are: phantom cars, buses, planes, houses, castles and battlegrounds. Under the right conditions, it becomes possible to see things that have happened in the past and sometimes even in the future.

Another famous case is that of the Flying Dutchman, which is said to appear off the coast of Africa's Cape of Good Hope.

Legend has it that in 1641, a Dutch ship sank during a violent storm in this region. The captain was said to have uttered a curse just before he died.

There have been several sightings of this ship, the most famous being by the Royal Navy ship HMS Bacchante in July 1881. The midshipman was later to become King George V and on board with him were his crew members and lookout man. It is reported that the lookout man had seen a 'strange light' and that the ship appeared to have an eerie glow. It is said that anyone who sees the phantom ship will die a 'terrible death'.

Not long after this, the lookout man fell from the ship's mast and died. Could this just be a coincidence, or a curse?

Possibly the most haunted coastline in Great Britain is the Goodwin Sands, a stretch of sandbank 8 km off Deal in Kent.

As many as 50,000 people are said to have been lost in shipwrecks in this region and ghost ship sightings are usually high and there are two particular ships that many people have reported seeing. The first, The Lady Lovibond, was lost on 13 February 1748. Since that fateful day she has been seen every fifty years. This ghost ship falls into the category of 'anniversary ghost'.

More than 100 years ago, a cross-channel paddle streamer, the SS Violet, hit the sands after a particularly violent storm.

There were no survivors and yet at the start of World War II, she was spotted by a lookout on the East Goodwin Lightship.

After an extensive search, nothing was found. This is an example of a 'random appearance'. The sands are also said to be the final resting place of a sunken island called Lomea. It is said that the sound of bells can be heard eerily tolling beneath the sea, seemingly from the lost churches of Lomea. There is no evidence to suggest that this island ever existed, but people have reported hearing these bells on several occasions, usually late at night during the winter months.

Mysterious Showers From The Sky:

Reports of bizarre showers of objects from the sky have been recorded for centuries. One of the earliest reports dates as far back as the second century AD, when the ancient Greek historian Athenaeus recorded a fall of fish that lasted for three days. Since then, inexplicable showers of fish, frogs, snakes, eels and even stranger objects such as coins have continued to fall.

In 1503, a rain of metal crosses was reported by Conrad Lycosthenes and Norway witnessed a fall of rodents in 1680.

Ice, ashes, sulphur, bricks, worms and the most macabre of all, blood and meat, have all fallen from the sky at one time or another. On 20 July 1851, at an army base in San Francisco, California, troops were showered with blood and pieces of meat that resembled beef. This grisly emanation occurred again on 1 August 1869 on a farm in Los Nietos, California.

Owner Mr J. Hudson found himself being showered with blood, hair and strips of meat whilst working outside. More recent cases were reported in Brazil in 1968, when blood and flesh fell from the skies, and similar phenomena have been reported many times since.

On 27 October 1973, two fishermen were battered by a sudden shower of pebbles that seemed to follow them as they ran towards their car and in 1984, there was a spate of mysterious falls of fish. In the borough of Newham, east London, a man in Canning Town found thirty fish in his garden and just one and a half miles away in East Ham, unexplained fish were found alive and, indeed, still falling from the sky. Meanwhile, in California, similar incidents were reported, with no evidence of a waterspout or a tornado occurring at that time. Just three years later, tiny frogs fell in Stroud in the Cotswolds during the month of October.

Phenomena such as this were recorded in Sumeria, Mesopotamia over 5,500 years ago. In those days, such objects falling from the sky were believed to be gifts from the gods.

Today, however, there are many explanations offered in an attempt to explain these mysterious showers. Charles Fort, researcher of anomalous phenomena, put forward the idea that the natural world was originally equipped for us by taking supplies that could be used as food and thus 'airlifting' them from elsewhere. Unlike the conventional scientific view that a phenomenon would be accepted as genuine only if it could be explained, Charles Fort believed that the fact the phenomenon had occurred and had been recorded was enough to prove its credibility.

Many scientists have examined reports of the strange phenomenon and many rational explanations have been offered. Ice showers have been blamed on faulty aircraft's de-icing equipment; however, this is unlikely, as many are so huge that they would have prevented planes from taking off in the first place. A lump of ice measuring 20 ft around its circumference and weighing half a ton fell on the Isle of Skye, Scotland, in 1849. Scientists claim other possibilities include objects being sucked from the sea by waterspouts and later deposited on land by the wind or by tornados, and frogs that have arrived in sand storms could have possibly been carried by atmospheric globules of water across land and sea.

Supporters of the paranormal claim that while these suggestions are plausible, they cannot account for every case.

There is no explanation as to why objects such as coins, blood and meat have fallen and on almost every occasion, there has been a clear blue sky when the showers have occurred. Charles Fort often spoke of his belief in a 'Super-Sargasso Sea in the sky', from where he claimed inanimate objects fell. The debate between scientists and paranormal societies still continues to this day. There may never be a plausible conclusion and so these mysterious showers remain just that.

Blood, Water And Tears:

Weeping Madonnas and statues of Christ that shed real blood continue to perplex many scientists and yet these types of phenomena have been recorded many times. In the 1950s, an Italian physician Dr Piero Casoli studied weeping Madonnas.

He reported that on average, they occurred twice yearly in Italy alone. Records of *The Fortean Times* magazine show that similar incidents have been recorded throughout modern history, with reports being made from all over the world.

In December 1960, a statue in a Greek Orthodox Church in Florida shed tiny teardrops and in 1974, a statue of the Virgin Mary wept in Sicily. In 1981, the same statue began to bleed from the right cheek. This strange phenomenon is one of controversy, as many of the stories could simply be dismissed as being mass hysteria and mass hallucination. Psychical researcher Raymond Bayless investigated such a case in New York between 1960 and 1966.

It began on 16 March 1960, when a portrait of the Blessed Virgin Mary began to weep tears inside its glass frame. The owner of the portrait, Pagora Catsoun, is called in her priest to examine the picture and he is reported to have witnessed another tear beginning to form in the left eye, which then slowly trickled down the face. News of the incident travelled fast and in the first week alone, 4,000 people visited the painting in order to pray, while tears flowed indefinitely. The painting was later transferred to St Paul's Cathedral, where it was enshrined.

Almost immediately after this account, another weeping Madonna turned up in the family, this time owned by the aunt of Mrs Catsounis, Antonia Koulis. Eventually, samples of the fluid were taken for analysis and they were found not to be human tears. The painting was also taken away and a replacement was given to Mrs Koulis. Once again, this, too, began to shed tears. Fascinated by these continuous occurrences, Bayless began his investigation in March 1966. He began to examine the painting more carefully and discovered that the stains below the eyes resembled crystallised particles of serum. He found no openings through which liquid could have been introduced and he therefore concluded that the substance was not liquid, but rather a dried globule, which remained in the same place. Bayless suggested that those who thought they had seen a tear descending from the eye had purely imagined it.

To date, one of the most famous reports of such phenomena is that of the bleeding Christ of Pennsylvania. In April 1975, Anne Poore of Boothwyn, Pennsylvania, USA, prayed in front of the plaster statue in her own home. She was shocked upon looking up at the statue to see that in the palms of its hands, tiny drops of blood had begun to form. When she eventually recovered from the shock, she moved the statue to her front porch, so that other people could see it. On Fridays and holy days, the flow of blood was particularly strong. After some time, the statue was relocated to St Luke's Episcopalian Church, where the pastor of the church Father Chester Olszewski witnessed it bleeding copiously for four hours.

Sceptics have come to see the statue and after examination, they came away convinced that the phenomenon was real. It wasn't long after that Dr Joseph Rovito, a respected physician, carried out his own investigation. No evidence of trickery could be found in the X-rays, but upon examining the blood, the doctor was astonished by the results. The low red blood cell count indicated a great age and yet the way in which the blood flowed from the statue indicated that it was fresh and fresh blood contains millions of red cells. Catholic priests concluded that this was, therefore, the blood of Christ.

As in this case, once trickery has been discounted, it is accepted that the liquid has materialised by way of teleportation. The regularity of such phenomena suggests that the teleportative force is created by an unknown intelligence and parapsychologists claim that it could be an unconscious response in the human mind, created when faced with a powerful image.

This paranormal phenomenon, in which events are linked to spiritual or psychological tensions, appears to take on two forms: religious phenomena and poltergeist activity. In both cases, the sudden manifestation can often be linked to a personal crisis; for example, it can occur during puberty or if there are feelings of sadness following the death of a loved one.

Pressures, frustration and inadequacy can also have the same effect.

An example that linked religious and poltergeist phenomena was in the case of devout Irish Catholic, with 16-year-old James Walsh of Templemore, Co. Tipperary. Holy pictures and statues within the home began to ooze blood and water also appeared in abundance in a hollow part of his bedroom floor. Every time it was emptied, it filled up again.

The ceiling was checked for any possible leaks, but none could be found. Furniture also moved by itself and the phenomena continued for quite some time. It appeared that the teenager was the main focus of the activity. Could this sudden manifestation be down to a combination of the family's profoundly religious beliefs and the sexual frustrations of a pubescent boy? The conclusion of such phenomena remains mystifying and an explanation has yet to be found.

19

Tips for Ghost Hunters

Before embarking on any investigation, be sure you are not trespassing and always get permission before entering private property. It is a good idea to familiarise yourself with the chosen location before you begin. Maps are often useful and drawing out a plan of the building and noting various rooms within it can also be extremely helpful. Gather as much information as you can prior to your visit; newspaper cuttings, articles, history books, and the Internet can all be sources of useful information.

When undertaking an investigation it is important to remember there are different types of ghostly manifestation.

Residual energies can remain within the building left by previous occupants and these can often be felt as either positive or negative energies. If visiting a location reputed to have an anniversary ghost, it makes sense to visit at the time that the ghost is said to appear. Spirits may also appear in 'orb' formation, so it is important to check the camera lens and the area for dust particles that may be misconstrued as orbs.

Most importantly, make sure you dress sensibly, as appropriate clothing is a must. Warm and waterproof clothing is best, as even in the summer months the temperature can drop late at night. A supply of food and flasks of hot drinks are also essential. Don't wear perfume or scent, as spirits will often communicate using smell. The presence of rose petal, lavender, pipe smoke and even unpleasant odours can indicate that a spirit is nearby.

Ready to begin? Below is an outline of a beginner's kit:

- Torch and extra batteries (ghosts are known to drain batteries).
- Notepad and pens.
- Recording equipment, such as a tape-recorder, Dictaphone or MP3 player (particularly useful if planning to conduct an EVP experiment).
- Video cameras (to record your experience).
- Camera (digital or flash will do; take several pictures, as you never know what you might see).
- Thermometer (the digital variety is preferable) to measure changes in temperature and to indicate 'cold spots'.
- Compass (to measure fluctuations in the magnetic energy field; a ghostly anomaly will tilt the needle to thirty per cent off magnetic north).
- Walkie-talkies (to communicate with others on the ghost hunt).
- Candle (for seances; also handy if the electricity fails or if the batteries die).

For those of you already familiar with ghost-hunts and vigils, you may be interested in learning about some of the equipment found in intermediate and professional kits. As well as containing many of the items found in the beginner's kit, there are some other interesting devices you might like to know about:

- EMF meters (the essential item for any pro, this equipment measures fluctuations in electromagnetic energy fields).
- Motion detectors (alerts to movement and subtle changes in pressure; to work effectively, the rooms they are in must be sealed off completely).
- EVP sound recorders (professional recording equipment used for experiments in electronic voice phenomenon).
- Digital camcorder with night vision (opens up the possibility for paranormal activity such as light anomalies, so they can be seen more easily).
- Infrared thermometer (these feature an alarm, alerting you to any sudden drops in temperature).
- Thermadata logger (measures changes in heat).
- Trigger objects (lay down a piece of paper, select an object and draw around it with a pen; then leave the area for a while and upon returning, see if it has moved).

Vigils:

Vigils can take place during daylight; however, conducting one at night is much more atmospheric. At the start of a vigil your senses will be heightened, especially if it is taking place late at night in pitch darkness. It is important to remember that sounds interpreted as being paranormal may just be the building cooling down. Bangs, creaking floorboards, etc., can all be confused with ghostly goings on. It is important to check out the area for draughts, as 'cold spots' may just be cold air coming from somewhere such as a door or window.

Before starting, check the building and surrounding area for any electromagnetic sources that may interfere with EMF equipment and locate any electrical wiring. Make sure all electrical/electronic equipment is switched off. It is not always possible to explore every room in the building, especially if you are investigating a large area, so splitting into smaller groups is a good idea, as it enables more ground to be covered. Stay in contact via walkie-talkie and make sure that all groups have a camcorder and a camera.

There are a number of methods you could try if you would like to make contact with a spirit. Scrying involves placing a lit candle in front of a mirror and staring at your reflection. It is said that spirits often communicate in this way, by changing your appearance to resemble theirs. Some people even claim that the room they are in also changes. If you are fortunate enough to have a medium present you could also try glass divination (placing your fingers on an upturned glass), automatic writing or a seance. It is important to note that these methods should not be attempted if a medium is not present.

At the end of your vigil, compare results and discuss how you thought the investigation went. Last but not least: have fun!

Bibliography and Recommended Reading

Acorah, D. *Haunted Britain & Ireland*, Harper Element Publishing Ltd, 2006

Barrett, F. *The Magus' of Celestial Intelligences*, 1801

Cheung, T. *The Element Encyclopedia of the psychic world: The Ultimate A-Z of Spirits, Mysteries and the Paranormal*, Harper Collins Publishers, 2006

Coleman, L. with illustrations by Jerome Clark. *Cryptozoology A to Z*, Fireside books, 1999

Collins, A. *The Black Alchemist*, ABC Books, 1988

Crowley, A. *Diary of a Drug Fiend*, 1922

Crowley, A. *The Book of the Law*, 1904

Crowley, A. *The Book of Thoth*, 1944

Crowley, A. *The Equinox*, 1909-1913

Ellison, Arthur J. *Science and the Paranormal: Altered States of Reality*, Floris Books, 2002

Eysenck, Hans J. and Sargent, C. *Explaining the Unexplained*, BCA Publishing Ltd., 1993

Ingram, John H. *True Ghost Stories*, Paragon, 1998, first published in 1886

Lévi, E. *The Dogma and Ritual of High Magic*, 1861

Linahan, L. *The North of England Ghost Trail*, Constable and Robinson, 1997

Moody, R. *Life After Life*, 1975

Natsis, C. EDS and Potter, M. 'Exploring the Unknown', *Readers Digest*, 1999

No single author responsible, *Marvels & Mysteries, Ritual And Magic,* Orbis Publishing Ltd, 1997

No single author responsible, *The Arabian Nights,*?

No single author responsible, *The Tibetan Book of the Dead,*?

Potts, T. *Discovery of Witchcraft,* printed by W. Stansby for John Barnes, 1613

Randles J. and Hough P. *The Afterlife: An Investigation into the Mysteries of Life After Death,* BCA Publishing, 1993

Randles, J. *The Complete Book of Aliens & Abductions,* Piatkus Books, 1999

Randles, J. *The Paranormal Source Book: The Comprehensive Guide to Strange Phenomena Worldwide,* Piatkus Books; New Ed edition, 1998

Randles, J. *UFOs and How to See Them,* Anaya Publishers Ltd, 1992

Ring, K. *Life at Death: A Scientific Investigation of the Near-Death Experience,* 1980

Spencer, J. and A. *The Encyclopedia of Ghosts and Spirits,* BCA by arrangement of Headline Book Publishing Plc, 1992

Stoker, B. *Dracula,* 1897

Stone, R. *Poltergeists and the Paranormal,* Blitz Editions, 1993

Underwood, P. *The Ghost Hunter's Guide,* Javelin Books, 1988

Webster, K. *The Vertical Plane,* Grafton Publishing, 1989

Whyman, P. *Phil Whyman's Dead Haunted: Paranormal encounters and investigations,* New Holland Publishers Ltd, 2007

Wilson, C. *Mysteries: An Investigation into the occult, the paranormal and the supernatural,* Duncan Baird Publishers, 2006

Wilson, C. *Poltergeist!* New English Library, 1981

Magazines and Journals:

Fortean Times, 2000

Grimsby Evening Telegraph, April 2000

Ireland's Own, 2003

Ireland's Own, 2004

Journal of The American Society for Psychical Research, October 2005

Metro, North-West Edition, Issues 17 November 2005 and 28 February 2006

Paranormal Magazine, Issue no.3, January 2006

The Times, 15 October 2005

Internet Websites

www.ufoseek.com/Area_51

www.bbc.co.uk

www.Fortean.Times.Magazine.co.uk

www.ghoststudy.com

www.ghostvillage.com

www.paranormalmagazine.co.uk

www.psychics.co.uk

www.hauntedchester.com